*And Then Comes
the End*

And Then Comes the End

David Ewert

Introduction by
Myron S. Augsburger

HERALD PRESS
Scottdale, Pennsylvania
Kitchener, Ontario
1980

Library of Congress Cataloging in Publication Data

Ewert, David, 1922-
 And then comes the end.

 Includes bibliographical references and index.
 1. Eschatology—Biblical teaching. 2. Bible.
N.T.—Criticism, interpretation, etc. I. Title.
BS2545.E7E9   236   79-28410
ISBN 0-8361-1921-5

AND THEN COMES THE END
Copyright © 1980 by Herald Press, Scottdale, Pa. 15683
 Published simultaneously in Canada by Herald Press,
 Kitchener, Ont. N2G 4M5
Library of Congress Catalog Card Number: 79-28410
International Standard Book Number: 0-8361-1921-5
Printed in the United States of America
Design by Alice B. Shetler

15 14 13 12 11 10 9 8 7 6 5 4 3 2 1

To my wife,
Lena,
who together with me awaits
"the appearing of the glory of our great
God and Savior Jesus Christ."

Contents

Author's Preface

The shape of things to come is of deep concern to many people in our day—both believers and unbelievers. One sign of the deep insecurity and the pessimism of the unbelieving world is the current interest in astrology. "But the danger is that Christians, experiencing this same sense of helplessness in face of world events, can replace astrology with biblical prophecy."[1]

There appears to be generally an apocalyptic mood in the Western world. Prophets of doom constantly remind us that with the current population explosion, the pollution of our environment, and the exhaustion of this world's food supplies, the end cannot be far away. And certainly these voices must be taken seriously. The church scene also reflects an almost feverish concern about the end. Bookstores are doing a brisk business as hundreds of thousands of readers snap up the latest paperbacks on prophecy. Many of the titles of these colorful publications have a sensational ring to them and elicit enthusiastic reader response.

These writings on prophecy might command more confidence if the writers all came to the same conclusions. While all of them (at least those in the evangelical stream) claim to base their studies on Holy Writ, they disagree widely in their findings, to the consternation of many devout Christian folk. One reason for this disagreement—one which many find hard to admit—is that the

Bible does not provide us with sufficient information to make it possible for its readers to plot the course of future events in precise detail. Perhaps even harder to admit is the fact that our understanding of what seems to be clearly stated in the Scriptures is limited and fallible.

This should, however, not lead us to an avoidance of the subject of eschatology (the teaching about future things). The Bible from beginning to end is eschatological; both Old and New Testaments look forward to the day when God will intervene in this world's history in a decisive way. Eschatology can, therefore, not be viewed as a mere appendage to the Christian faith. Hope is the very essence of our Christian life. While evangelicals may not agree on the details as to how this hope is to be realized, all agree that at the heart of the blessed hope is the expectation that Christ will return in great glory to usher in the age to come.

Throughout history there have been those whose curiosity led them to develop rather detailed structures of the last days. Such time-schemes are intriguing to some believers; others find them confusing. Much more serious, however, is the fact that disagreements over side-issues in eschatology often lead to deep divisions among Bible readers. What is more, those items which are not so clearly taught in the Scriptures are often pushed into the center. This endangers the deep unity of faith which should be enjoyed among all those who confess the Bible to be their ultimate authority in matters of doctrine. When certain methods of biblical interpretation are equated with the Bible itself, then anyone who interprets the Bible differently is considered unbiblical.

While this author has no desire to encourage controversy, the problems in eschatology which divide believers today will not go away by sweeping them under the rug. The better one is informed on the subject the better one can understand why equally devout students of the Bible do not always see eye to eye.

The following pages reflect the writer's present understanding of the teachings of the New Testament on matters pertaining to the end-times. Whereas other positions, with which the writer disagrees, are mentioned here and there, he has tried not to be polemical. The following chapters, much rather, attempt to lay out in a non-technical way the major themes of New Testament eschatology. The simplicity of the approach to the various topics may help serious Bible readers see that eschatology is not a topic that can conveniently be left either to scholars or to cranks. Rather, eschatology is very relevant for one's daily life as a follower of Jesus.

The writer's interest in this area of biblical thought was deepened when some years ago he began teaching New Testament theology to seminarians—a subject in which eschatology quite naturally constitutes the final chapter. Interest in publishing some of these materials was stimulated by the response of readers to a series of articles published by the author on this subject in a denominational paper. These chapters are sent forth with the hope that they will, in the words of Hebrews 10:25, encourage "one another, and all the more as you see the Day drawing near."

David Ewert
Fresno, California

Introduction

History is still in the hands of God. This is the basic affirmation of eschatology. God continues to be at work in history, as He was in the past. Eschatology is the projection of that same work of God into the future. The Christian's hope is the affirmation of faith that the God who has worked in the past is not capricious but will work consistently in the future. The true prophet, or seer, is one who sees into the future or speaks into the future on the basis of God's actions in history. Our ability to be prophetic is contingent upon our understanding of the way God has been at work in history.

In this significant book, *And Then Comes the End,* David Ewert has rendered yeomen's service to the church. To prepare a significant new work on future events is not an easy task, especially since none of us will agree on every point. The careful scholarship demonstrated in this book is an achievement of distinction in contemporary literature on eschatology. Many popular authors on prophecy in recent decades have been so committed to an extreme dispensationalism, and/or a flat-book view of the Bible, that the reader is left without a clear understanding of the ultimate meaning of Christology as the interpretation of the acts of God in history, past and future. Ewert has dared to do something different. He has demonstrated integrity in his scholarship and his method of interpretation. He broadens our awareness of that which is yet to come until we see the grand harmony of all future events with "that blessed hope, and the glorious appearing of the great God and our Saviour Jesus Christ."

A unique aspect of this book is the way in which Ewert maintains the tension between the prophetic and the apocalyptic. This important perspective holds the message before us as the Word of God for today in the midst of the continuing conflict between the Lamb and the beast. The fact that the kingdom is being experienced by "the rule of Christ" is as prominent as the conviction that this kingdom will be actualized in the fullness of His future role. We can pray "Thy kingdom come, Thy will be done on earth as it is in heaven" expecting this to be answered for our daily living as well as in our anticipation of the parousia.

Because of its prophetic comments on contemporary living, this book does not easily fall into the mold of any one of the traditional systems of interpreting eschatology. The author's insights will challenge and enrich persons who stand in any of the systems.

Whether or not you agree with every detail of Ewert's presentation, I invite you to enter into dialogue with him and allow the Spirit of God to speak to you through the pages which follow. I thank God for the diligence, the scholarship, and the spirit communicated in this book. I sincerely believe that this volume will enrich the faith of the broad range of Christians and enhance our sense of mission "to occupy until He comes."

As you consider the message of this book, remember the words of the Apostle Paul regarding his own statements on eschatology, "Comfort one another with these words."

Myron S. Augsburger, President
Eastern Mennonite College and Seminary
Harrisonburg, Virginia

CHAPTER ONE

"The Last Days"

Everywhere today one hears believers say, "We are in the last days." If one probes a little deeper it becomes obvious very soon that the term "the last days" is not understood in the same way by everyone. There are those who confidently proclaim that the last days began in 1948, with the establishment of the modern state of Israel, and that God will wrap up this present age no later than 1980. It may well be that the last trumpet will sound no later than 1980—or earlier for that matter. But what about all those faithful followers of Jesus through the long centuries of the Christian era who also believed that they were living in the last days? Were they wrong? Our answer would depend on how we understand the term "the last days." In this first chapter, then, we intend to examine what the New Testament means by "the last days," and to consider the imminence of the end of this age.

The Meaning of the "Last Days"
The Beginning of the "Last Days"
According to the prophets of old, the new age was to be inaugurated by the outpouring of God's Spirit upon man (Is. 32:15; 44:3; Ezek. 36:25-27; Joel 2:28). Peter saw the fulfillment of these hopes (specifically that of Joel) in the outpouring of the Spirit at Pentecost (Acts 2:17). With the coming of the Spirit, the

last days had begun. F.F. Bruce, in commenting on Acts 2:17, puts it this way: "The 'last days' began with Christ's first advent and will end with his second advent; they are the days during which the age to come overlaps with the present age."[1]

The coming of the Spirit was the capstone of the Christ-event, and so it is equally correct to say that the last days were inaugurated with the birth, death, and glorious exaltation of Christ. The prophets, writes Peter, wondered about the time of Christ's coming (1 Pet. 1:10 f.), but now that Christ has been manifested "at the *end of the times*" (1 Pet. 1:20), this is clear.

Paul, writing to the Corinthians, states that "the end of the ages" have met in the apostolic age (1 Cor. 10:11). While God spoke in many and various ways in the past, says the writer to the Hebrews, "in these last days he has spoken to us by a Son" (Heb. 1:2). The same writer speaks of "the powers of the age to come" (Heb. 6:5) which are being experienced by the believer today. Also, with reference to Christ's first advent, he affirms that Christ "has appeared once for all at the end of the age" (9:26). All these passages witness to the conviction of early Christianity that the last age had dawned with the incarnation, passion, and resurrection of Christ.

John in his first Epistle tells his "little children" twice that it is the last hour (1 Jn. 2:18). The "last hour" is used here in the sense of "the last days."[2] The new age had dawned with the coming of Christ, and so Christians knew that they were living in the last days. "Early Christians," says Marshall, "certainly regarded the whole period between the first and second advents of Jesus as constituting the last days. ... Now that the last period in world history had been inaugurated by the coming of Jesus, it could not be long before the end."[3] Of course, the present evil age was still very much in existence, but as Paul puts it, Christ delivered "us from the present evil age" (Gal. 1:4). Whereas the church knows that the powers of darkness are still at work, "the darkness is passing away and the true light is already shining" (1 Jn. 2:8).

John R. Stott, writes: "All Jews were familiar with the division of history into 'the present age' and 'the age to come' (cf. e.g. Mt. 12:32), and the New Testament teaches that 'the age to come' came with Jesus. He inaugurated it, so that the two ages overlap one another."[4]

This period in which the two ages overlap was, however, viewed as transitional. The "last days," which began with Jesus and the outpouring of his Spirit (Acts 2:17; Heb. 1:1, 2; Jas. 5:3), or the "last times" (1 Pet. 1:20; 1 Cor. 10:11) were viewed as lasting only for a period of time, and then they would come to an end. The age to come had broken into history, and therefore this present age was drawing to a close. "The form of this world is passing away" (1 Cor. 7:31). The interim between Christ's first and second coming would not last forever. The "last days" were to end when the "last day" arrived (Jn. 6:39, 40, 44, 54; 11:24; 12:48); the "last times" would end with a "last time" (1 Pet. 1:5).

Many evangelical Christians think of the last days as the final epoch just before the end. The New Testament, however, equates them with the new era introduced by Christ's work of redemption accomplished at his first advent. We can say that Christians throughout this interim have lived and are living in the last days. Believers always live, as it were, "between the times."

That this interim would last as long as it has (or may yet last) was not known to the New Testament writers, for the day and the hour of the consummation of this age was hidden in God. God is not bound by our clocks and calendars—which are human inventions. But we know on the authority of his Word, that these last days in which the church lives will come to an end.

The Consummation of the "Last Days"

While the New Testament church had the deep conviction that the "last days" had begun with the coming of Christ and the outpouring of his Spirit, the Spirit was also seen as the guarantee that these last days would not last forever. For this reason the Spirit is called the "first fruits" of the harvest that is yet to come (Rom. 8:23), and the "down payment" on the inheritance into which we are yet to enter (Eph. 1:13-14). "Through the Spirit . . . we wait for the hope of righteousness" (Gal. 5:5).

We must then distinguish clearly between the "last days" and the "last day." Our Lord spoke repeatedly of the "last day." "And I will raise him up at the last day" (Jn. 6:39, 44, 54) is our Lord's promise to those who believe in him. Martha, in the midst of her grief at the death of Lazarus, still clung firmly to the hope that "he will rise again in the resurrection at the last day" (Jn. 11:24), and Jesus did not question that hope. Jesus warns that "on the last day" (Jn. 12:48) his word will judge those who reject him.

Another way of speaking of the "last day" is to call it the consummation, the wrap-up (*sunteleia*). Jesus' disciples on one occasion asked the Master: "Tell us, when will this be, and what will be the sign of your coming and of the close of the age?" (Mt. 24:3). Notice here the connection between the coming of Christ and the consummation of this age! Jesus himself had spoken several parables that focused on the "close" of the age (Mt. 13:39, 40, 49). The last words of Jesus in Matthew's Gospel are: "Lo, I am with you always, to the close of the age" (Mt. 28:20). "The close of the age" is a Jewish phrase found in the New Testament only in Matthew's Gospel.[5]

Sometimes the last day, the consummation, is called simply "the day" (1.Thess. 5:5; 1 Cor. 3:13; Heb. 10:25). The background for this term is the Old Testament shorthand "the Day," for the "the Day of the Lord" (cf. Mal. 4:1). At other times the demonstrative is added and we get it in the form of "that day" (Mt. 7:22; Lk. 10:12; 2 Tim. 1:12, 18). It is also called "the great day" (Jude 6; Rev. 6:17; 16:14). More commonly, especially in Paul, the last day is called "the day of the Lord" (1 Thess. 5:2; 2 Thess. 2:2) or "the day of God" (2 Pet. 3:12; Rev. 16:14). And since Jesus was called "Lord" by early Christians, the Old Testament term "day of the Lord" was easily recast and becomes "the day of Jesus Christ" (1 Cor. 1:8; 2 Cor. 1:14; Phil. 1:6, 10; 2:16).

Occasionally the character of the day is denoted by such phrases as "the day of judgment" (Mt. 10:15; 11:22, 24; 12:36; 1

Jn. 4:17; 2 Pet. 2:9) or "the day of wrath" (Rom. 2:5). But it is also a "day of redemption" (Eph. 4:30). It is the day when the "last" trumpet will sound (1 Cor. 15:52) and the "last" enemy (death) will ultimately be overcome (1 Cor. 15:26).

This last day is also called simply "the end" (*telos*). Jesus in his apocalyptic discourse recorded in Mark 13 warned, "When you hear of wars and rumors of wars, do not be alarmed; this must take place, but the *end* is not yet" (v. 7). Prior to the "end," the gospel is to be preached in all the world (Mt. 24:14). According to 1 Corinthians 15:24 the end will come when Christ delivers the kingdom over to the Father after vanquishing all evil powers.

We see, then, that the "last days" began with Christ, but the "last day" is yet to come. The "end times" were inaugurated with Christ's coming, but the "end" has not yet come. When the consummation of this present age will occur we do not know, and Jesus forbade his followers to speculate: "It is not for you to know times or seasons which the Father has fixed by his own authority" (Acts 1:7). What then do we do with the many passages in the New Testament which state that the end, the consummation, the last day, the coming of Christ, is near? Let us see what the New Testament has to say on that!

The Imminence of the "Last Days"
The Closeness of the End

The New Testament writers quite obviously held that the coming of the Lord was near. Paul lived and served with the consciousness that "the appointed time has grown very short" (1 Cor. 7:29). While some commentators see in this a reference to the crisis in Corinth, others take Paul's reference to the brevity of time to refer to the return of Christ. Writing to the Romans he reminds them that "salvation is nearer to us now than when we first believed; the night is far gone, the day is at hand" (Rom. 13:11, 12). (Whether Philippians 4:5, "The Lord is at hand," has a strictly eschatological meaning is not quite certain.)

Other apostolic writers share Paul's view that time is hastening to the end. "The end of all things is at hand," says Peter (1 Pet. 4:7). The perfect tense (*engiken*) puts the emphasis on imminence and immediacy. James writes: "Establish your hearts, for the coming of the Lord is at hand" (Jas. 5:8). The writer to the Hebrews exhorts his readers to encourage one another and this "all the more as you see the Day drawing near" (Heb. 10:25). "For our author," says F.F. Bruce, "as for the other New Testament writers, 'the day' is primarily the final phase, the day of Christ's parousia."[6]

John, too, stresses the imminence of the end. "Children, it is the last hour," he writes (1 Jn. 2:18). The Book of Revelation begins and ends with the reminder that "the time is near" (Rev. 1:3; 22:10). Whatever the duration of this time of waiting may be, the end is always near. Another way in which John stresses the imminence of the end is to say that the things which God had revealed to him about the future will take place "quickly" (*en tachei*: Rev. 1:1; 22:6— 2:16; 3:11; 22:7, 20; *tachu*: tachometer is based on the root of the word used here.) "I come quickly," is our Lord's word of assurance to the suffering saints of Asia Minor.

If a preacher today should announce as his topic: "Behold, I Come Quickly," or "The Coming of the Lord Is Near," he would, more likely than not, want his audience to understand that the Rapture will take place soon. What he may have overlooked, however, is that these words were spoken in the first century, and therefore must have the same meaning in the 20th century as they did in the first.

One could, of course, take the rather questionable position that Jesus and the apostles were in error when they predicted the imminent end of this age. But once we make ourselves the judge of what in the Bible is trustworthy and what is not, we lose all ground under our feet. The better approach is to inquire whether the New Testament writers did not speak of the closeness of the end in a way that makes sense even today, some 1,900 years later.

One way of reading the texts that speak of the imminence of Christ's return is to say that when God's hour strikes then things will happen quickly. Or one could read the word "quickly" in the sense of "certainly." Moreover, the word "quickly" may suggest that God is in control of history. The suddenness with which God acts is a sign of his power. "And the Lord whom you seek will *suddenly* come to his temple" (Mal. 3:1). "And *suddenly* there was with the angel a multitude of the heavenly host praising God" (Lk. 2:13); "And *suddenly* a sound came from heaven like the rush of a mighty wind" (Acts 2:2). Nothing stops God from acting when the time has come and the final hour has struck.

While we do not want to discount these ways of reading those passages which speak of imminence, it appears to us that a better approach is to understand them as expressing the primitive church's understanding of time (*urchristliches Zeitgefuehl,* as it is called in German). In the presence of eternity, time shrinks together; the perspective is abbreviated. A thousand years are viewed as a day (2 Pet. 3:8). To say that the time is near is to summon us to the outermost ramparts of time, to the point where time is fulfilled, to the moment when history ends and the new morning begins to shine, which is no longer of this world.[7]

The church always lives in the twilight just before the dawn of the eternal kingdom. Robert Mounce writes: "The tension of imminence is endemic to that span of redemptive history lying between the cross and the parousia."[8] If imminence is understood in this way, then the message of the New Testament remains relevant for all generations. Then believers always live on the borderland between this age and the age to come.

One saying of Jesus, which appears in different forms in the Synoptic Gospels, regarding the imminence of his return has puzzled Bible readers through the centuries. In his apocalyptic discourse recorded in Mark 13:30 Jesus says, "Truly, I say to you, this generation will not pass away before all these things take place" (cf. Mt. 24:34). One question is: Does "generation" (*genea*) mean people or a period of time? If it means people, as the context seems to favor, then we must ask: Did he mean the human race? The Jewish people? The Christians? This "sort of" people? Or, did he mean his contemporaries? The latter seems to be the meaning, and is so understood by commentators such as Lagrange, Bruce, Lane, Cullmann, and others. This, however, is the most difficult meaning of "generation," for then Jesus is saying in effect that the people living in his day would yet see the end of the age—which they did not.

Some commentators resolve the problem by limiting "all these things" (*tauta panta*) to the destruction of Jerusalem, which Jesus' generation would witness some 40 years later. Still others take "all these things" to refer to the return of Christ at the end of the age, but as foreshadowed in Jesus' generation in the events leading up to the destruction of Jerusalem. The prophet Joel saw the day of the Lord in a current locust plague, but beyond the locust plague lay the day of the Lord at the end of the age. Similarly, then, Jesus' contemporaries would witness the cataclysmic events leading to the destruction of Jerusalem, but that cataclysm was but a prototype of what would happen at the end of the age many generations later.

Entirely fanciful is the view that the last days began in 1948, and since a generation is 30 or 40 years long (taking *genea* in a temporal sense), one can predict with some degree of accuracy the date of our Lord's return. People who do such calculations should not stop reading at Mark 13:30, but read on to verses 32 and 33 in which Jesus says, "But of that day or that hour no one knows, not even the angels in heaven, nor the Son, but only the Father. Take heed, watch; for you do not know when the time will come." (That the early church preserved this saying in which Christ's own knowledge about the "end time" seems to be limited, makes it all the more trustworthy. While Luke omits "nor the Son," and many manuscripts omit it in Matthew 24:36, it is secure in Mark.)

The Problem of the Delay

The apostles have been charged with error for teaching that they were living in the last days and that they expected the Lord to return in their lifetime. Indeed, some New Testament scholars argue that some of the teachings of Jesus were deliberately recast by the apostles as the awareness of the fact that the church might continue on earth for some time grew upon them.[9] Others have tried to show there is a gradual decline of hope in the imminent return of the Lord in the letters of Paul. That however is somewhat hard to prove, for even in the pastoral epistles hope still burns brightly (cf. Tit. 2:11 ff.). On the other hand, in 1 Thessalonians (which may be the earliest letter of Paul extant), Paul takes into account the possibility of dying before the rapture takes place: "Whether we wake [live] or sleep [die] we might live with him" (1 Thess. 5:10).

Hand in hand with the hope in the first-century church, of the imminent return of Christ, there are also clear indications that there was to be an interim between the two comings. And this expectation of an interim was not simply born out of a delay of Christ's return, but was anticipated by Jesus. It is, for example, inherent in the commission to go into all the world and preach the gospel to every creature (Mt. 28:19-20). One can see it also in the comments Jesus made about the loving act of the woman who poured the costly ointment on him: "And truly, I say to you, wherever the gospel is preached in the whole world, what she has done will be told in memory of her" (Mk. 14:9). That would take time!

This twofold attitude of the believers regarding the return of Christ—that it is near, and that it may yet be far away—has characterized the church's time of waiting from the first century up to the present (and it must continue to do so). It is for this reason that we have repeated admonitions in the writings of the New Testament to remain calm and to wait patiently for Christ's coming. "We wait for it with patience," says Paul (Rom. 8:25). The farmer, as James has it, "waits for the precious fruit of the earth, being patient over it. ... You also be patient ... for the coming of the Lord is at hand" (Jas. 5:7-8). Indeed, Christ will return a second time "to save those who are eagerly waiting for him" (Heb. 9:28).

Already in the first century there were those who made mockery of the Christian hope of our Lord's return (and they are still with us). As the time of waiting was extended, they asked: "Where is the promise of his coming?" (2 Pet. 3:4). Clement, in his first letter, written toward the end of the first century, warns against those who say, "We have heard these things even in our fathers' times, and, see, we have grown old and none of them has happened to us."[10]

Peter gives a threefold answer to these scoffers: (a) God's Word was fulfilled in the past, and so it is reasonable to expect the promise of his coming to be fulfilled in this instance as well (2 Pet. 3:5-7). In Noah's day, too, the scoffers argued that things would always remain as they are, but they were caught off guard when the Flood came. And just as there was a flood of water, so there will be a flood of fire when the end comes. (b) God does not measure time the way we do. "With the Lord one day is as a thousand years, and a thousand years as one day" (v. 8). "God sees time with a *perspective* we lack; even the delay of a thousand years may well seem like a day against the backcloth of eternity. Furthermore, God sees time with an *intensity* we lack; one day with the Lord is like a thousand years."[11] (c) The reason this time of waiting is extended is that God is forebearing and does not wish that any should perish, but that all should come to repentance (v. 9). God's grace is extending the day of salvation. Therefore, while the church prays, "Come, Lord Jesus!" (Rev. 22:20), it thanks God for every day of grace that he gives to humankind.

Living in the "Last Hour"

Since we do not know the time of Christ's return, the passages which speak of the imminence of his coming speak powerfully to Christians living in every age, for they always live in the last hour. And just as the apostolic writers pointed to the closeness of the end to underscore watchfulness, so must we. Every living believer must be prepared to face the end either through death—should the Lord tarry—or at the return of Christ. On the one hand, he can say with Paul, "We who are alive . . . are left until the coming of the Lord" (1 Thess. 4:15). On the other, he can confidently affirm, "We shall not all sleep, but we shall all be changed" (1 Cor. 15:51).

There is a dual emphasis throughout the New Testament on the "already" and the "not yet." There is an awareness of a time of waiting in which the church is to carry out the Great Commission, but there is also a lively expectation of the coming of the Lord. This tension between the "already" and the "not yet" explains many of our conflicts with the world in which we live. Whereas we have tasted of the powers of the age to come, we are still beset by evil powers. "The Christian hope is that God who has begun to rule in Jesus Christ will one day rule openly over all men. The present interim period will come to an end. The era of evil will cease, and God will establish a new heaven and a new earth characterized by righteousness."[12]

We have the assurance that if we walk by the Spirit we will have victory over sin, but we know that we can never attain to perfection in this life. God has revealed his mysteries to us (1 Cor. 2:6 ff.), but our understanding of God's purposes is still very restricted (1 Cor. 13:10).

Because we are still "on the way" and have not yet arrived, we must also be modest in our claims about our spiritual experiences. We experience salvation here in this age only as a foretaste; we are "being saved" (1 Cor. 1:18); and we hope for "salvation" (1 Thess. 5:8). Our Christian life is marked by many "lows" though God in his mercy may give us an occasional "high."

Included in this tension between the "already" and the "not yet" is also our bodily existence. So often our spirit is willing but the flesh is weak. We grow tired and weary, and we become ill, and some day, should the Lord tarry, we will die. We are confident, however, that he who has begun the good work in us will bring it to completion in the day of Jesus Christ (Phil. 1:6). "History is moving towards the goal of the great and final 'coming,' when that which is ambiguous and fragmentary will be done away. The exodus will end in the arrival in the promised land; the exile will end in the return; the pilgrimage will end in homecoming."[13]

To live in the last days means to sniff the air of the world to come. It means to live on tiptoe, spiritually. Without the awareness that we are always living in the last hour life becomes flat and insipid. Excitability isn't called for, but the kind of expectancy that says to us when we go to bed at night, that before morning breaks the eternal morning may have dawned.

Discussion Questions

1. What event or events mark the beginning of the last days? Is there a difference between what some Christians mean when they say, "We are living in the last days," and what the author intends? Check out Acts 2:17; 1 Peter 1:20; 1 Corinthians 10:11; Hebrews 1:2; 9:26.

2. What are some of the words and phrases used in Scripture to refer to the end of this age? See John 6:39; Matthew 24:3; 1 Thessalonians 5:5; Jude 6; 2 Peter 3:12; Matthew 10:15; Romans 2:5; Ephesians 4:30; Mark 13:7.

3. Suppose someone said to you, "If Christ were going to come again as he promised, he would have done so by now. Therefore, he must not be coming again." How would you respond? How does the author account for the period of time which has transpired between Christ's first and second comings? What guarantee do we have that this "interim period" will not last forever? See Romans 8:23; Ephesians 1:13, 14; Galatians 5:5.

4. See Mark 13:30. What does "all these things" refer to? How was this prophecy fulfilled? Is there more to be fulfilled? What are some of the lines of reasoning used to interpret this passage?

5. Should it make any practical difference to Christians that they believe they are living in the tension between the "already" and "not yet"? How?

CHAPTER TWO

"What Will Be the Sign of Your Coming?"

Writing in *Christianity Today*, W. Dyrness refers to a series on biblical prophecy which appeared in 1958, in which the evangelical contribution concluded with this paragraph: "The study of Bible prophecy is difficult but rewarding. God has revealed many facets of His plan. How thrilling it is to watch events as they unfold, and see the working of His mighty hand." The writer then calls upon believers to watch for these events, these signs of the times.[1]

No one doubts that the subject of prophecy is complex; few Christians dispute the value of it. And, to be sure, God has revealed many facets of his plan. Were it not so, we would be hard-pressed to muddle through the darkness of this age. However, when it is claimed that one can tell how close to midnight we are on God's time-clock, by observing signs on the political, economic, or religious horizon, we must call for sobriety.

A question most hotly debated among evangelical believers is whether it is possible to establish with some degree of accuracy how far along on the historical continuum humankind has come by observing the "signs of the times." "Signs of the times" is a biblical phrase, to be sure, but how is it to be understood?

When Jesus predicted the destruction of Jerusalem, his disciples asked him, "Tell us, when will this be, and what will be the sign of your coming and of the close of the age?" (Mt. 24:3). (This is the only place in the New Testament where Christ's coming is identified with the end of this age. It is worth noting, for some hold that this age will continue even after Christ has come.) In response to their query Jesus gives them a number of signs of the "end times." Let us keep in mind, however, that the entire period of history, stretching from the first to the second advent of Christ, are the last days, and therefore the signs which Jesus gives must be understood as characterizing this entire interim.

Since this has not always been observed, Christians throughout the centuries have tried again and again to infer from current events, which they identified as "signs of the times," how close the end of the age was. We mention several of these misguided attempts, for they serve as a warning.

Mistaken Interpretations of "Signs"

As early as the second century Montanus had come to the conviction that the end was near and announced to his followers that the New Jerusalem was about to come down from heaven on Asia Minor. Many abandoned their possessions, even broke family ties, in order to prepare for this great event—only to be disappointed.[2]

Such speculations were not confined to unorthodox Christians, for Cyprian (third century) of Carthage wrote: "The day of pressure is even over our heads, and the consummation of all things and the coming of Antichrist approaches."[3]

In the sixth century Gregory the Great declared in one of his sermons:

> Of all the signs described by our Lord as presaging the end of the world, some we see already accomplished. ... For we now see that nation rises against nation. ... Earthquakes overwhelm countless cities. ... Pestilence we endure without interruption. It is true that as yet we do not behold signs in the sun and moon and stars; but that these are not far off we may infer from the changes in the atmosphere.[4]

Scholars have pointed out that the expectations of the end of this age became rather intense in the Christian world as the year AD 1000 drew near. Some have questioned the evidence for this, but it looks from all appearances that such calculations will increase as we near the end of the second 1000 years after Christ. It is well for us to remember that our calendar is a human invention, and that God is not guided by such conveniences.

About the middle of the thirteenth century William of Saint Amour wrote *The Perils of the Last Times,* in which he proclaimed the end of the world on the basis of what he saw happening in his day.[5]

These speculations continued during and after the time of the Reformation. Since the Roman pope had come to be thought of as Antichrist, there was nothing in the way, it seemed, of Christ's imminent return. John Wesley followed the Pietist Johann Bengel in expecting the overthrow of the "Beast" in 1836. Bengel did not live long enough to discover his error.

William Miller, the founder of the Millerites of America, was not quite so fortunate. He interpreted the 2,300 days of Daniel 8 as years (a highly questionable approach), and by taking 457 BC as his starting point, he reached 1843 as the date of Christ's advent. When that failed he postponed it for a year. His followers sat dressed in white on hills and housetops waiting for the great event to occur, but were disappointed. One of the branches of the Millerites are the Seventh-Day Adventists.[6] Miller's misguided effort illustrates that one cannot only misread the signs of the times but also the Scriptures.

A similar nineteenth-century movement was led by Claus Epp, Jr., a Russian Mennonite farmer-preacher. He believed that the tribulation spoken of in Revelation was imminent. This view was prompted by the Russian political situation which threatened to rob the pacifist Mennonites of some privileges, especially exemption from military, which they considered vital to their faith. Confident that God was going to provide a refuge for the faithful in Turkestan, Epp led a group of 600 Mennonites by wagon train from Southern Russia and the Volga River region eastward to the wilderness of Asiatic Russia. They expected to meet the Lord there in the year 1889. Some of Epp's disillusioned followers eventually found their way to North America. Others stayed on, and thousands of their followers remain in the same region today. This story of fanaticism, hardship, and disillusionment is told in *The Great Trek*, by Fred Richard Belk (Herald Press, 1976).

C.I. Scofield, through whose Bible notes the teachings of John Darby became popular in America, was deeply convinced that World War I marked the beginning of the final conflict which would bring this age of grace to an end. He wrote in *The Sunday School Times* (Oct. 17, 1914):

> Armageddon is to be fought, not on the fields of France or Germany, but around Jerusalem, on the plain of Esdraelon, and Idumea. If, then, Turkey and the Balkan States shall be drawn into the war now raging—then we may confidently answer that the war which is now drenching France, Poland, Belgium, and Germany with torrents of human blood, on a scale, and with a remorselessness never before equalled in human history, does indeed mark the beginning of the end of this age.[7]

This view was shared by many others, and it should not surprise us, for there had never been such a conflagration in human history. But the end did not come.

Leonard Sale-Harrison felt that the end would come in 1940 or 41, because of what he thought was the revival of the Roman Empire under Benito Mussolini. Today many see the sign of the end in the European Common Market.

More recently Charles R. Taylor proposed September 6, 1976, as the date of Christ's coming. He takes 1948 as his starting point, the year in which the modern state of Israel was established. He then interprets our Lord's promise, "This generation shall not pass away until all these things take place," to mean the generation following the establishing of the state of Israel.

Allowing 35 years for a generation, he arrives at the year 1983. From that he substracts 7 years, for he holds that there will be seven years of tribulation after the Rapture, and so arrives at 1976 for the Lord's return.[8]

It is exactly this kind of speculation that discredits prophecy. Many sincere Christians turn away in disgust and leave the subject to cranks. If we are to believe that Christ's coming is very near because of the establishment of the state of Israel in 1948, then what did the imminence of the Parousia, (Christ's second coming) mean to the Christians through the centuries when there was no such a state?

All such attempts arise out of the conviction (misguided, we think) that current events can be made to match biblical prophecies. On what grounds, for example, can it be said that modern Russia is the Gog and Magog of Ezekiel 38 and 39, and that therefore the end must be near? (Interestingly, in Revelation 20:8 Gog and Magog represent the evil forces that attack the city of God after the millennium, not before.)

But are there then no signs that might alert us to the imminence of the Parousia? Indeed there are, but they are the kind of signs that make sense in any generation, in the first century as well as the last. Let us give some examples!

Signs of the Times for All Times

There is considerable disagreement among biblical scholars on the number of signs mentioned by our Lord and his apostles. In a recent booklet by A. Skevington Woods, *Signs of the Times* (Baker, 1970), eighteen such signs are listed. We want to restrict ourselves to a few, which may serve as examples.

Deception

Jesus warned that the end-times would be characterized by deception. False Christs would rise and lead many astray (Mk. 13:5, 6 and parallels). The warning is repeated in Mark 13:22: "False Christs and false prophets will arise and show signs and wonders, to lead astray, if possible, the elect."

Paul wrote to Timothy: "Now the Spirit expressly says that in later times some will depart from the faith by giving heed to deceitful spirits and doctrines of demons, through the pretensions of liars whose consciences are seared" (1 Tim. 4:1, 2).

Paul's prediction, however, does not mean that there were no deceivers in Paul's day. What is predicted for the future in prophetic utterances is often conceived of as already operative in the present.[9] Peter is equally emphatic: "There will be false teachers among you, who will secretly bring in destructive heresies. . . . And many will follow their licentiousness. . . ." (2 Pet. 2:1, 2). In this, however, he sees history repeating itself, for he begins by recalling that there were false prophets in Israel, too. "There always have been and there always will be false teachers among the people of God."[10]

Similarly John in the Revelation says of the beast from the land that "by the signs which it is allowed to work in the presence of the beast [from the sea], it deceives those who dwell on earth . . ." (13:14). This was happening in the Asiatic churches while John wrote. False teachers have been present throughout the Christian era and will continue to be present right up to the end. Justin Martyr (second century) recalled Jesus' warnings about deceivers in his *Dialogue with Trypho the Jew:* "In the interval before His second coming, there would, He warned them, be heresies and false prophets arising in His name."[11]

The deception of the saints that we are witnessing in our day is frightening. We are surrounded by a chaos of cults. And it has been asked, seriously, whether much of what is published today in the name of prophecy does not fall into the category of what Paul condemns as the desire for "teachings which tickle the ears." That, too, as he suggests, is a sign of the last days (2 Tim. 4:3). Of course there were deceivers already in the first century. It would be hard to say how close we are to the end by pointing to the profusion of cults (not to mention the occult). The need for watchfulness is as great today as in the day of Christ and the apostles.

War

A second sign of the end-times mentioned in Mark 13 is war. "And when you hear of wars and rumors of wars, do not be alarmed; this must take place, but the end is not yet" (v. 7). The disciples were not to think that when war broke out, as it did in AD 66, that the end was imminent. The entire interim preceding the return of Christ was to be marked by war. The first apocalyptic rider which John saw riding across the pages of human history had a bow and "he went out conquering and to conquer" (Rev. 6:2). And the one that followed him, on a bright-red horse, was to take away peace from the earth, "so that men should slay one another; and he was given a great sword" (6:4).

While there have been long periods of peace in some parts of the world, war has been the tragic lot of humankind throughout history. The year 1914 marked the beginning of the first world war, and another followed shortly thereafter (1939-1945). With the dropping of the first atomic bomb, the threat of total annihilation has hung over our planet like the sword of Damocles. Christ's followers seek to preserve, not destroy, life. They do what they can to establish peace, yet the church must be prepared to live and to work in the midst of a war-torn world until the day comes when nations will learn war no more (Is. 2:4).

There are those who are convinced that a third world war would mark the end of this age. That may well be, but it would be rash to proclaim this as biblical truth. While there is no doubt that history is moving to a final showdown between God and the forces of evil, it would be presumptuous to predict that the next war will be Armageddon (Rev. 16:16). War remains a sign of the times until our Lord himself appears with the armies of heaven to make an end of all rebellion against God (Rev. 19).

Earthquakes

Jesus mentions earthquakes in answer to the disciples' question about the signs of the end (Mk. 13:8). Earthquakes have occurred throughout the Christian era, swallowing up entire cities with their inhabitants. Of late earthquakes seem to have increased in frequency. Or is it that the seismograph and the television screen have made us more conscious of their frequency and their terror? The Book of Revelation, which portrays the end-times with apocalyptic imagery, mentions earthquakes no fewer than five times (6:12; 8:5; 11:13, 19; 16:18).

We do not know how many earthquakes we will yet witness before the end comes, but every tremor is God's reminder that the existence of all earth-dwellers is insecure. Every quake is a call to mankind to turn to God in repentance before the day comes when he will shake the earth and the heavens (Heb. 12:26).

Famine

Jesus mentions famine together with earthquakes (Mk. 13:8). Famine is a frequent aftermath of war, and the rider that follows the one who brings bloodshed (Rev. 6:4) rides on the black horse of famine (Rev. 6:5, 6). Famine is often caused by natural catastrophes, such as drought. Much of the hunger of our world, however, is due to humankind's own mismanagement of nature's gifts. But whatever may be the causes, famine is a sign of the end-times. From the time of Agabus, who predicted a famine in the reign of Claudius (Acts 11:28), until the return of our Lord, when we will hunger and thirst no more, there will be famines. The forecasts of world-famine are frightening. Some scientists fear that, should this earth escape a nuclear holocaust, it may end with an exhaustion of its food supplies. We do not know.

Meanwhile, Christians must be in the forefront in bringing relief to the hungry. Those who ask in the final judgment: "Lord, when did we see thee hungry?" receive the answer: "Truly, I say to you, as you did it to one of the least of these my brethren, you did it to me" (Mt. 25:37, 40).

War and famine and earthquakes, said Jesus, were the beginning of travail (Mk. 13:8). Jesus may have had in mind the destruction of the Jewish state in the foreseeable future. Yet, these phenomena are also the birth pangs which precede the birth of the eternal kingdom and which characterize the interim between the cross and the crown. Christ's followers, therefore, must be prepared to face a turbulent world with faith and confidence.

Persecution

This is another sign mentioned by Jesus (Mk. 13:9, 11-13). The church will always be under fire. With varying degrees of intensity, persecution has been the lot of the church in every century. Jewish tribunals, the persecutions of the Caesars, the tortures of the Inquisition, the blood of the Anabaptists at the time of the Reformation, the concentration camps of Siberia, and the recent martyrs of Uganda tell the story of the way that leads from the cross to the crown.

There has never been an age when Christians somewhere in the world have not suffered for their faith. Christians thank God for every country that has freedom of religion, and they do not deliberately make martyrs of themselves. Yet, they know that "all who desire to live a godly life in Christ Jesus will be persecuted" (2 Tim. 3:12)—if not by sword and thumbscrew, then by ridicule or job-discrimination.

Mission

Another sign, of quite a different order, which Jesus mentions is the preaching of the gospel to all nations (Mk. 13:10). "God has mercifully provided this 'interval' before he makes a final end of the old era, so that all men may have the opportunity of hearing the gospel and becoming citizens of the new era (Mk. 13:10; 2 Pet. 3:9)."[12] Mark 13:10 stands between two verses which speak of persecution (vv. 9, and 11 f.), as if to suggest that the resistance which the church will experience from the world is often prompted by her evangelistic efforts. In any case, before the end comes, the good news must be preached to all nations. The consummation will not take place until the mission of the church is complete.

This does not mean, however, that we can tell by the size of the missionary force or by other statistics, how close to the end of the age we are. It is as Cullmann writes: "The gospel must be preached by the Church in every generation as a sign of the approaching end. But the Church cannot calculate the date of the end, nor hasten its coming by fulfilling this duty which is assigned to it in the divine plan."[13]

We have mentioned half a dozen signs of the times; others could be added. These signs were given to the disciples of Jesus to assure them that, in spite of the darkness of the present age, God will fulfill his purposes; and in spite of suffering and tragedy the church must never lose sight of its mission.

It may come as a surprise to some readers that we have not included the establishment of the state of Israel as a sign of the times. The reason for this omission is a simple one: the New Testament nowhere foresees the reestablishment of the state of Israel. The burden of the New Testament writers is to show that Jew and Gentile are now one in Christ. The promises to Old Testament Israel are seen as fulfilled in the church. To be sure, Paul does hold out hope to the people of Israel in Romans 11:25-27, but it is the hope of salvation and not of national restoration. Every Jew that is going to be saved must be saved in the same way as the Gentile. It is as G.E. Ladd puts it: "Possibly the modern return of Israel to Palestine is a part of God's purpose for Israel, but the New Testament sheds no light on this problem."[14]

The signs of the times are not like road signs which tell us how many miles we are from our destination. So much of today's prophetic preaching is of that nature, and often the biblical message of the blessed hope is smothered by interpretations of current events. But the increase in false cults, the rumors of global warfare, the devastating earthquakes, the hungry masses, or for that matter, the great progress in evangelism, cannot conclusively give us information on how close we are to the end. These signs of the times span the entire age of the church; they are signs which we must always regard as God's call to lift up our heads, for our redemption draws nigh.

Discerning the Times

Jesus accused his adversaries on one occasion of failing to interpret the signs of the times. "You know how to interpret the appearance of the sky," said Jesus, "but you cannot interpret the signs of the times" (Mt. 16:3). Surrounded by evidence that God's new age had dawned in the Person and work of Jesus, they were still looking for signs. It is dangerously easy to get caught up in the attempt to interpret current events in the light of prophecy and not to discern the times at all. Could the rash of books on the end times, with one author outdoing the other in sensational claims, also be a sign of the times? Can these not easily become a convenient instrument in the hand of Satan to sidetrack us from our true mission in the world?

Our Lord said that the last days would be like the days of Noah before the Flood. They ate and drank, married and gave in marriage (Mt. 24:37 ff.). I have heard these verses expounded as referring to the gluttony, drunkenness, and sexual permissiveness of the days of Noah. And since these evils plague our society as well, the end must be near, it is argued. But eating, drinking, and marrying are all legitimate and essential activities. The problem of Noah's contemporaries was that they did not discern the times in which they lived. They were completely immersed in earthly pursuits; not their drunkenness, but their secularism, hedonism, and materialism proved fatal. If that is so, we are well advised to apply this passage to ourselves, rather than to figure out how close we are to the end by the number of divorces or by the amount of liquor consumed in the United States and Canada annually.

Moreover, preoccupation with the darkness of our times—war, famine, earthquakes, immorality, witchcraft—can plunge us into defeatism. It can lead to a determinism which is pagan in character and far removed from what Jesus and the apostles mean when they call us to watchfulness. If war is a sign of the times, should we then stop working for peace? If famine is the fulfillment of prophecy, shall we then not give our bread to the hungry? If "men's love will grow cold" in the last days (Mt.

24:12), shall we do nothing about renewal? I have heard it said (on the basis of Revelation 3), that the lethargy of the church is a sign of the times—as if we had entered the Laodicean period and there was little we could do about it, since it is predicted. But that is fatalism, not faith.

C. S. Lewis warned that belief in the second coming of Christ must never preclude "sober work for the future within the limits of ordinary morality and prudence ... happy are those whom it finds laboring in their vocations, whether they were merely going out to feed the pigs or laying good plans to deliver humanity a hundred years hence from some great evil. ... No matter; you were at your post when the inspection came." [15]

Between the inauguration of the last days with the coming of Christ and the outpouring of the Spirit and the return of Christ, the church lives "between the times." This interim has been expanded into a period of nearly 2,000 years. While many are certain that we will not reach the year 2000 before our Lord returns, we have no authority to make such predictions. God has fortunately given us enough light about the future so that we can live and serve and suffer with joy and confidence during this time of waiting, until the day dawns and all the shadows flee away.

Discussion Questions

1. Enumerate some of the signs of the end times given by Jesus. See Mark 13:3-13. Note how these signs are expounded in the following texts: 1 Timothy 4:1, 2; Revelation 6:2, 5, 6, 12; 2 Timothy 3:12. Were these signs present during the first century of the church? Are they present today?

2. Recall some of the persons in church history who led movements based on the return of Christ at a predetermined time. Why were these movements a failure? What events and personalities in the twentieth century have been associated by some as signs of the end time? Why is it risky to interpret current events as signs of the end time?

3. The author gives two principles of scriptural interpretation in this chapter: One, signs of the end times must be interpreted in such a way as to make sense to the first century as well as the twentieth. Two, promises made to Israel in the Old Testament are to be interpreted as finding their fulfillment in the church. Do you agree with these principles? What difference does it make in interpreting the Bible? Why doesn't the author include the reestablishing of the state of Israel as a sign of the end times?

4. What should be the response of the Christian to such signs of the times as war, famine, earthquakes, and apostasy?

CHAPTER THREE

"In the World You Have Tribulation"

The last days which span the time between the first and second advent of our Lord are days of divine grace and patience. They are the days in which the church fulfills the Great Commission to bring the gospel to every creature. As God's rule is extended over the lives of men and women, and as God calls people out of darkness into his marvelous light, the evil one puts up stiff resistance. He sees his dominion over the lives of people threatened. This leads to conflict and calls for suffering on the part of God's people. Any treatment of the doctrine of the "last things" must, therefore, take the suffering and tribulation of the church into account. Suffering characterizes the life of the church throughout the last days which began with Pentecost and which will end with his Parousia.

When the entire New Testament witnesses to the fact that the church is called to suffering in this world, it is hard to understand how some influential preachers in America can speak of the Christian life as if it were one great success story. One hears it glibly proclaimed that if Jesus' followers will only live right, attend church regularly, and give their tithes, God will prosper them materially and even keep them from physical ill and distress. Indeed, it is said, if America would only return to God, there would be no more poverty, no crime, and no fear of Russia.

Are we to understand, then, that the many thousands of saints in other parts of the world who live in poverty all their life are not faithful? And do we mean to say that the many who have suffered and died for the cause of Christ did not live right? Where in the New Testament do Jesus and the apostles promise believers they will be spared from want and suffering?

Helmut Thielicke, after a lecture tour in America, was surprised that the most important question of our time, that of suffering, had never been asked during the many question-and-answer periods in which he had participated. Americans, he writes in retrospect, think only of eliminating suffering (which, of course, has its place), but not of accepting it. [1]

In Judaism it was held that the days preceding the coming of Messiah would be very dark and troublesome—the birth pangs of the messianic age as they were called. Similarly in the New Testament Jesus and the apostles speak of tribulations that are to precede the return of the Son of man in glory. The perspective has changed, for in the eyes of the apostles the Messiah had come, but the notion that dark days precede the return of Christ remains. While on the one hand the believer rejoices that he has been delivered from the present evil age (Gal. 1:4), he knows also that he must redeem the time "because the days are evil" (Eph. 5:16). Let us see what the New Testament has to say about these days of trials and tribulations which precede the age to come!

Tribulation Predicted by Jesus

So closely is the follower of Jesus bound to his Lord that he cannot expect better treatment from the ungodly than did Jesus. Jesus affirmed this when he said: "If they persecuted me, they will persecute you" (Jn. 15:20).

In the Sermon on the Mount Jesus concludes his series of Beatitudes by calling those who are persecuted for righteousness' sake "blessed" (Mt. 5:10). He amplifies this by adding: "Blessed are you when men revile you and persecute you and utter all kinds of evil against you falsely on my account" (v. 11). Since the other Beatitudes describe what every disciple is to be, it must be concluded that Jesus expected his disciples to be despised and rejected, slandered and persecuted. This, it seems clear, "is as much a normal mark of Christian discipleship as being pure in heart or merciful."[2]

Before sending out his disciples to preach the message of the kingdom, Jesus prepared them by predicting that they would be delivered up to councils, flogged in synagogues, dragged before governors and kings for his sake (Mt. 10:17, 18). Addressing the multitudes in Galilee Jesus said, "If any man would come after me, let him deny himself and take up his cross and follow me" (Mk. 8:34).

In his farewell discourses to his disciples Jesus declared: "In the world you have tribulation," and then added the comforting word, "but be of good cheer, I have overcome the world" (Jn. 16:33). Although his followers may suffer and die, they will never become the prey of evil powers.

Perhaps nowhere did our Lord elaborate on the sufferings of his followers as in his Olivet discourse (Mk. 13; Mt. 24; Lk. 21). His followers, he said, would experience the sorrows of wars, earthquakes and famines; but these were to be "but the beginning of the birth-pangs" (Mk. 13:8). The sufferings which Palestinian believers would have to endure in the wars leading to the destruction of Jerusalem (AD 66-70) were to be but a foretaste of what the church was to experience throughout this interim in which it carries out its mission. Jesus predicts that his followers will be hated by all for his sake (Mk. 13:13). And these sufferings will end only when the Son of man comes in the clouds with great power and glory (Mk. 13:26).

Not only the prophetic words of Jesus, but also his example led his followers to expect sufferings. From his earliest ministry in Galilee Jesus encountered fierce resistance to his message and deeds. But steadfastly he went the way of the cross until, in the end, they put him to death in the most shameful way. One of the major lessons he tried to teach his disciples was that the Messiah had to suffer and die—something that was completely contrary to popular Jewish expectations.

Immediately after Peter had confessed at Caesarea Philippi that Jesus was "the Messiah," Jesus began to teach his disciples that the Son of man must suffer many things (Mk. 8:29-31). As if to correct any false notions about the way in which the Messiah was to establish his kingdom, Jesus makes it plain that suffering was included in the divine plan of redemption. Moreover, the salvation of the world—the victory over sin, death, and evil powers —could not be achieved by political greatness, nor by the power of the sword, but by the cross and suffering. If his kingdom were of this world, he told Pilate, then his servants would fight. But since his kingdom was of a different order, he had to suffer.

We have to remember that at the heart of the Christian gospel is a cross. The ground plan for the salvation of the world was cruciform. If the kingdom was established by Jesus at such an awful cost, then it can be expected that the extension of his kingdom by his followers will be attended by suffering and tribulation. And that is exactly what happened when the church was established at Pentecost.

Suffering Experienced by the Early Church

As one turns to Luke's record in Acts of the life and work of the early church, it becomes obvious very quickly that the lot of the early believers was not easy. They were boycotted, ostracized, slandered, abused, and even killed. At the beginning of Acts we see Peter and John leaving the council, "rejoicing that they were counted worthy to suffer dishonor for the name" (5:41), and at the end of the book Paul is a prisoner of imperial Rome. Had Gamaliel's counsel in the Sanhedrin gone unheeded (5:33-39), the Jerusalem church may well have been obliterated. The death of the Hellenist, Stephen, however, sparked a bloody persecution. Spearheading this violence against the church was Saul, who sought desperately not to make martyrs of his fellow-Jews, but to turn them back to the faith of the fathers. He was not successful, so he pursued them to their death, binding and delivering to prison both men and women (Acts 22:4).

By God's grace this persecuting rabbi met the risen Christ on his way to Damascus, and was made an apostle. When the Lord called him to take the gospel to the Gentile world, the Lord warned Paul he must suffer much for his sake (Acts 9:16)—a prediction fulfilled rather fully. Not only in Damascus was a plot against Paul's life discovered, but also in Jerusalem. We can only imagine the sufferings he endured when for fourteen years he witnessed for his Lord in Syria and Cilicia. Much of what he recounts in that long catalog of suffering in 2 Corinthians 11:23-28 must have happened during those so-called "silent years."

It is not necessary for us to recount all the experiences of suffering recorded in the Book of Acts. Think only of Paul's stoning at Lystra, of the beating he and Silas got in Philippi, and how with lacerated backs and their feet in the stocks they sang praises to God! Recall Paul's flight from Thessalonica under cover of darkness, his day in court in Corinth, the riot in Ephesus, his capture in Jerusalem, his long imprisonment in Caesarea, and finally his journey to the capital as a Roman prisoner! In a very literal way Paul bore in his body the marks of Jesus (Gal. 6:17).

We should, of course, remind ourselves that Paul was not the only one to suffer for his faith. Stephen had died before his very eyes (Acts 7); Peter was imprisoned; James was killed with the sword (Acts 12:1, 2). If we are to trust some of the extra-biblical traditions about the apostles, then it appears as if most of them died a martyr's death.

Moreover, let us not forget the sufferings of the many nameless saints who made up the early church, who faithfully witnessed for their Lord. Paul recalls, for example, that the Thessalonians had received the word "in much affliction, with joy inspired by the Holy Spirit" (1 Thess. 1:6). The same can be said for many of the other churches founded by the apostles. All of the apostles who have left us something in writing assume everywhere that the church is called to suffer.

Tribulation Anticipated by the Apostles
The Many Kinds of Trials

Wherever one turns in the letters of the New Testament, one is struck by the great diversity of testings the early believers had to endure. Peter in fact speaks of "various trials" (1 Pet. 1:6). The Greek adjective "various" (*poikilos*) means colorful or variegated. The eschatological tenor of the context of this verse ("the last time," v. 5, the "little while," v. 6) underscores the insistence of the New Testament that the last days are to be marked by a great variety of sufferings.

Paul, in listing some of his own sufferings, mentions imprisonments, beatings, lashings, stoning, hunger, thirst, and other trials endured for the sake of the gospel (2 Cor. 11:23-28). The writer to the Hebrews reminds his readers of the struggles they had when they became Christians: exposure to abuse and affliction, imprisonment, and plundering of their own property (Heb. 10:33, 34). Romans 8 closes with the great affirmation that neither "tribulation, or distress, or persecution, or famine, or nakedness, or peril, or sword . . . nor anything else in all creation, will be able to separate us from the love of God in Christ Jesus our Lord" (8:35-39). The early believers experienced the whole gamut of trials: from the loss of friendship to the loss of life itself.

It is natural, then, that many of them found it hard to come to terms with suffering. Aside from the natural aversion to pain and loss, it appears that some had a hard time harmonizing their trials with the confession that Jesus was Victor. He had triumphed over all evil powers at the cross, thereby defeating Satan. Why, then, could his followers not share in this triumph? As most of us do when we experience trials, they were asking whether God was punishing them for some misdemeanor on their part perhaps. Some may have even become resentful, thinking that God was treating them unfairly.

The apostles addressed these questions relating to tribulation, and out of their statements emerges a theology of suffering. We now turn to this subject.

The Significance of Suffering

First, to suffer is a way of imitating Christ, we are told. Paul explains to the suffering Thessalonians that those who had killed Jesus were the ones who now persecute the church, and so they were following in Christ's way (1 Thess. 2:14-16). Suffering slaves are reminded that Christ also suffered, leaving them an example "that you should follow in his steps" (1 Pet. 2:21). As the teacher writes a line which the student is to copy, so Christ provides an example, giving the suffering slave, who in that day was hardly above the animal, a great dignity.

Paul has a deep desire to experience the "fellowship" of Christ's sufferings (Phil. 3:10). Elsewhere he speaks of a fellowship in the gospel, a fellowship of the Spirit, a fellowship at the Lord's table, a fellowship in giving. But there is also a profound fellowship with the Christ in his suffering. Christian legend later had it that Paul became so conformed to Christ in his suffering and death that people could see the wounds of Jesus in Paul's body. One can discount that bit of medieval mythology, but certainly he carried in his body the dying of the Lord Jesus.

Paul knew that the redemption of the world had been accomplished by Jesus' death. But he also realized that if the good news of redemption was to reach the world, Christ's followers would have their full share of the sufferings of Christ (Col. 1:24). Christ continues to suffer in his members. Perhaps Paul also felt that the more he suffered for Christ the less his fellow-Christians would have to endure. F.F. Bruce is of the opinion that "Paul accepted his injuries and trials the more readily in the hope that thus his converts and other fellow-believers would be spared the like."[3]

To be sure, believers do not share equally in Christ's sufferings, but no one should think that he or she has been exempted from trials for the sake of Christ. Tribulations in the church are the continuation of the sufferings of Christ.

Paul got a glimpse of this truth when he was overwhelmed by the light from heaven on the way to Damascus. The voice from heaven asked: "Saul, Saul, why do you persecute me?" The sufferings of the church on earth are felt by the head of the church, Christ (Acts 9:5).

Second, Paul claims that suffering, like faith, is a gracious gift from God (Phil. 1:29). To suffer without fear is a sign for the believers that they will ultimately triumph, as it is a sign of defeat for their adversaries (Phil. 1:28). The Thessalonians are told that God has "ordained" (*keimai*) them for suffering (1 Thess. 3:3-5). Peter reminds suffering servants that God has called them to suffer (1 Pet. 2:21).

Third, not only is there nothing shameful about tribulation (Eph. 3:13), but through trials God teaches his children many valuable lessons. Paul confesses that his trials in Asia had been so severe that he nearly despaired of life. In retrospect, however, he sees at least two benefits which come to him from this period of testing. One, he learned not to trust in himself but in God. Second, it equipped him to comfort others who got into similar troubles (2 Cor. 1:3-11).

Moreover, "suffering produces endurance, and endurance character," as Paul says (Rom. 5:3-4). Testings come from the hands of a loving Father who treats us as true children. And while discipline is painful, "later it yields the peaceful fruit of righteousness to those who have been trained by it" (Heb. 12:11). Peter likens trials to the fire that tests metal, consuming the dross and leaving pure gold behind (1 Pet. 1:7). There is, therefore, much to be gained for the disciple of Jesus by suffering. Those who comfort the ill and the sorrowing should, of course, refrain from speaking glibly about the great benefits the patient is deriving from his pains. Of all the mysteries of life, suffering is probably one of the greatest. Nevertheless, the Scriptures confirm that God is able to affect growth and refine character through suffering. What, then, should the believers's attitude be toward tribulation?

The Christian's Attitude Toward Tribulation

First, tribulation should not surprise the believer, as Peter says (1 Pet. 4:12). Gentile Christians in the Roman world would

find it utterly strange that anyone should suffer because of his religion—much like people in the free world find that strange. So
Peter counsels that trials should not be viewed as a strange mis-
fortune. On the contrary, the believer is to rejoice in the privilege
of having fellowship in the sufferings of Christ (v. 13), and count
themselves happy (*makarios*) when they are reviled for the name
of Christ (v. 14). Believers must expect to share in the Messianic
woes, the birth pangs of the new age.

Second, what is important is that the suffering saints stand
firm and endure their trials and not become disloyal to Jesus
under pressure (1 Thess. 3:2, 3). The great word for Christian
endurance under persecution is *hypomone* (literally "to remain
under the load"). This means more than passive resignation to the
inevitable, but speaks of a joyous acceptance of tribulation as the
preliminary stage of God's eternal kingdom. In the Book of
Revelation *hypomone* is repeated seven times to indicate what the
believers' attitude must be at the end of this aeon.[4]

Third, a temptation that no doubt came to many a believer
when he was innocently accused and abused was to pay his
enemy back in kind. But that, explains Paul, is not the way Jesus'
followers should act. "When reviled, we bless," says Paul; "when
persecuted, we endure; when slandered, we try to conciliate"
(1 Cor. 4:12, 13). Peter counsels those suffering innocently to
"take it patiently" and then holds up Christ as model: "When he
was reviled, he did not revile in return" (1 Pet. 2:18-23). What is
more, Christ entrusted himself to the One "who judges justly" (v.
23). Just as Christ committed himself and his cause into God's
hands (with an allusion to the Suffering Servant of Isaiah 53:3), so
the suffering believer can commit his cause to the One who in the
end will set the records straight.

Fourth, as an encouragement to endure sufferings for Christ
patiently, the apostles hold out high rewards to those who remain
faithful to the end. The sufferings of the present, writes Paul, "are
not worth comparing with the glory that is to be revealed to us"
(Rom. 8:18). "If we endure, we shall also reign with him" (2 Tim.

2:12). And James holds out the promise of the crown of life to those who endure testings patiently (Jas. 1:12).

Fifth, Christians are encouraged to rejoice in suffering. This strikes us as paradoxical, but the reason for joy is that trials are the road by which the saints go to glory. Just as Christ suffered and then went to glory (1 Pet. 1:10, 11), so his followers, after suffering a little while, will enter into glory (1 Pet. 1:6, 7). Peter himself was a witness to the sufferings of Christ, but also one who was given a foretaste of "the glory that is to be revealed" (1 Pet. 5:1). Believers, then, can be glad when trials come, for that is but the preliminary step to the gladness that will be theirs "when his glory is revealed" (1 Pet. 4:13). This association of joy and suffering, however, is not limited to the writings of Peter. One finds this also in the sayings of Jesus (Mt. 5:12), the writings of Luke (Acts 5:41), Paul (1 Thess. 1:6), the writer to the Hebrews (12:2), James (1:2), and others.

Tribulation was so much a part of the early church that the apostles devote a lot of attention to it. Suffering, however, was to be the lot not only of the early church, but was to characterize the life of the believer throughout history until Christ's Parousia. For that reason the trials of the church can be called eschatological sufferings. Nowhere is this underscored more heavily than in the last book of the Bible.

Tribulation, the Christian Way of Life

The Revelation to John was written by one who was exiled to Patmos because of his testimony for Jesus. He shares with his readers not only the tribulation but also the kingdom and the patient endurance in Jesus (Rev. 1:9). Indeed it is because Christ has begun to reign that John is able to endure the tribulation. "Kingdom" is the divine alchemy that transforms tribulation into triumph, and so it can be endured with patience.

All the churches of Asia are exhorted to stand firm in their trials, for great rewards await those who "overcome." The overcomer in Revelation is not one who overpowers and defeats his persecutors, but one who overcomes by the blood of the Lamb and by the word of his testimony and who, because of his loyalty to Jesus, is willing to die (12:11).

Nowhere, however, is it said that the church suffers the wrath of God which is poured out on the wicked "earth-dwellers" who take the side of the Beast. The three series of seven judgments on sinful humanity are John's way of portraying the judgments of God in history. Since the believers live in the world in the midst of the godless, they too have to suffer in these judgments. But instead of the mark of the Beast, they have the seal of God upon them. All those who have his seal (chaps. 7 and 14) are protected in the judgments that strike this world from time to time prior to Christ's return. When famines, earthquakes, wars, and revolutions strike, the saints suffer along with the ungodly, but they are never forgotten by God; he brings them to glory in the end.

The souls under the altar ask: "Lord ... how long?" (Rev. 6:10). They are told to rest a little longer until the number of the martyrs is complete. Moreover, they are given white garments as a sign that they have triumphed. From that vision John's readers were to learn that, should they be asked to go the way of the cross, as other martyrs had, they could be certain that it leads to the crown.

This is typical of the entire Book of Revelation. Scenes of suffering are interlaced with promises of God's protection and final glory. All of the Lamb's followers have God's seal on them. They are his own and he protects them. In chapter 7 John sees these suffering saints coming home to glory in an endless stream. "These are they who have come out of the great tribulation" (7:14), he is told.

In chapter 11 we have a scene in which God's witnesses are killed, but God raises them up and takes them to heaven (11:12). It has been said that the church, like her Lord, may die on Good Friday but rises again on Easter Sunday. The Beast makes war on the saints because they refuse to accept his mark (Rev. 13:7), and so John calls the church to endurance and faith (v. 10). People who have to suffer for their faith understand Revelation much more easily. It was written with tears, and only with tears is it understood.

The church must always be prepared for suffering during the entire span of time between the first and second coming of Christ. This does not mean that it tries to make a martyr of itself. Peter warns us against suffering because of our own misdeeds. Also, the church is thankful to God for long days of peace. Indeed, it prays that it may lead a peaceable life (1 Tim. 2:1 ff.). But at any moment the forces of wickedness may subject Christ's followers to suffering and death.

Most Bible readers who have some knowledge of the church's history know that suffering has attended the church's life throughout this interim between the cross and the crown. But there are those who hold out the hope to the church that it will be spared the especially severe tribulation at the end of this age. This view calls for some comments.

The "Great" Tribulation

A very popular view of the tribulation is that before the Antichrist emerges, God will rapture his church and spare his people the severe testing at the end of this age. This idea was first suggested by John Darby (ca. 1838). In the view of this writer, such an interpretation is hard to defend from the New Testament passages that speak of tribulation. The one text that promises deliverance from the great tribulation (Rev. 3:10) is simply an assurance to the believers that they will not succumb in the judgments of history that befall "the earthdwellers," that is, the wicked.

The teaching that the church will be raptured before the End is rooted not in the New Testament, but is inferred from Daniel 9:24-27. It is argued that God's plan with Israel was interrupted by the church age and that after the church is removed, Daniel's 70th week (seven years) will follow—a period of great tribulation under the rule of Antichrist. Chapters 4-18 of the Revelation are then said to describe the terrors of this seven-year period of tribulation. But it seems strange that a major portion of a New Testament book should have nothing to say to the life of the readers to whom John addressed it, or for that matter to all the saints through the ages who have found comfort in this book. It may be added, that it is always precarious to interpret the New Testament in the light of the Old. The apostles teach us to interpret the Old in the light of the New.

Also, it seems difficult to argue for a pre-tribulation rapture when 2 Thessalonians 2:3 explains that the Lord will not come "unless the rebellion comes first, and the man of lawlessness is revealed," whom Christ will liquidate at his Parousia (v. 8).

Peter Beyerhaus holds that the notion the church will be raptured before Antichrist emerges is an assault against the message of Christ's Parousia. Even evangelical preachers are guilty of this assault.

> This assault consists of emphasizing the return of Christ without taking notice of the beacon that signalizes the most crucial eschatological event before his coming: the revealing of "the man of lawlessness" (2 Thess. 2:3-12). . . . The Christian Church on earth is not going to be united with its Head before it has passed the final, almost super-human test of being confronted with the apocalyptical temptation by Antichrist. Therefore the widespread teaching of a rapture that dodges this serious reality must be refuted as a dangerous distortion of New Testament eschatology.[5]

We are ill-advised to hold out the hope to the church that, before the night of this age gets too dark, Christ will take us away from the trials of life. Missionary David Adeney, who has spent half a lifetime in Asia, observes that when tribulation came upon the church in communist China, it was caught off guard. This was the case because missionaries in China had taught that the church would be spared the tribulation.[6] Any interpretation of biblical prophecy that exempts the church from persecution or tribulation should be rejected.[7]

In a later chapter we will argue that the Scripture nowhere teaches two separate aspects of Christ's return, between which the great tribulation can be inserted. This point has been cogently argued by Robert Gundry, of Westmont, in his book: *The Church and the Tribulation*.[8]

Suffering has been a mark of the true church throughout the ages. "Indeed all who desire to live a godly life in Christ Jesus will be persecuted" (2 Tim. 3:12). Americans sometimes wonder whether there is much genuine Christianity left in countries under totalitarian regimes. Conversely, Christians who have to suffer for their faith in these lands, wonder at times whether there is much genuine Christianity in the free West, since there is so little suffering. George Ladd writes, "To be sure, we experience little hostility in America, indeed, in many cities, it is good for one's business and social standing to be a member of a certain church. This has lulled many Christians to sleep in the feeling that God would not possibly allow his people to suffer such a devastating persecution."[9]

Let us, therefore, put on the whole armor of God, that we may be able to stand in the evil day!

> And when the strife is fierce the warfare long,
> Steals on the ear the distant triumph-song
> And hearts are brave again, and arms are strong.
> Alleluia!

Discussion Questions

1. How should we respond to the popular notion that becoming a Christian results in material prosperity and escape from adversity? What did Jesus have to say which refutes this notion? See Matthew 5:10, 11; 10:17, 18; Mark 8:34; 13:8, 13; John 15:20; 16:33.

2. The author says that at the heart of the Christian gospel is a cross. Is this a reference only to Christ's death? Or does it have implications for the life of the Christian? If yes, how? Consult

Mark 8:34; Romans 12:12, 14, 17, 19-21; Philippians 3:10; Colossians 1:24; 1 Peter 2:21.

3. How do you explain the fact that most Christians in the West do not suffer for their faith? Is it a sign of unfaithfulness? Under what circumstances might Christians in Canada and the United States be subjected to persecution? Would we be prepared to suffer?

4. Where in the world are Christians suffering because of their faith? Why? How can we identify with their plight?

5. Tertullian, the early church father, said the blood of the martyrs is the seed of the church. Why is it that the church often grows—in numbers and depth of commitment—under adversity? What are some of the other positive outcomes of suffering for the sake of Christ? See Romans 5:3, 4; 8:18; 2 Timothy 2:12; Hebrews 12:11; James 1:12; 1 Peter 1:6, 7.

6. How should we respond to suffering? Look up 1 Corinthians 4:12, 13; 1 Peter 4:12-14. Note especially the assuring words of Paul in Romans 8:35-39.

CHAPTER FOUR

"O Death, Where Is Your Victory?"

Death, it has been said, is the only unmentionable subject left in these outspoken times. Ignoring death, however, does not make it go away. George Bernard Shaw reportedly made the observation that the statistics about death are very impressive: one out of one dies. Yet until recently we've been tiptoeing around death as if ignoring it would make it go away.

When we were children we played funeral, as did the children of Jesus' day (Mt. 11:16, 17). Since we never missed a funeral in our community, death was very much a part of our life. Today some medical scientists are taking an intense interest in the subject of death and dying, but most people try to avoid the topic. This is the worst possible attitude that one can take, for there is nothing that affects our life as much as death. We may not find it hard to accept the fact of death as such, since we are constantly reminded of it by our environment. But to recognize that some day *I* will die, lifts the subject out of academic abstraction.

"Death, then, is not something that confronts man at the end of life's journey, but is with him throughout life, affecting his way of looking at reality and challenging the meaning he sees in life."[1] Physically, man dies like the beast. However, it is precisely in the fact that man knows he must die that he is different from the beast.

What makes the subject of death so solemn is the fact that man's existence does not end at the grave. The awful finality with which death ends our earthly life is shattering enough. Even the secularist who holds that death is the end of man's existence, cannot really face death with equanimity. The realization that our eternal destiny is determined by how we respond to Christ in this life makes death an even more serious fact.

The Christian, then, must always live with a twofold expectation: death and the return of Christ. While all believers would prefer to be alive at the coming of the Lord, they must always confess with David of old: "But truly, as the Lord lives ... there is but a step between me and death" (1 Sam. 20:3). Because of our individualism, it's probably true for most believers that the threat of death is more real than the expectation of the Parousia of Christ.

In a later chapter we shall have more to say about Christ's coming; in this chapter we want to face the question of death and the intermediate state between death and the return of our Lord. The New Testament writers have much to say about death, but relatively little about the intermediate state. Could it be that they were so hopeful that the Lord would come in their lifetime that they paid less attention to the existence of the believer in the interim between death and the coming of Christ?

The subject of this chapter, then, is twofold: we want to make some comments on death by which our earthly pilgrimage is brought to an end; then we want to see what information we can gather from the pages of the New Testament about the intermediate state.

Death, the End of Earthly Existence
The Power of Death

Ever since the fall of man, man has lived his life under the sign of death. Death is the lot of every person. Our bodies are mortal (Rom. 6:12; 8:11; 1 Cor. 15:53). Only God has immortality (1 Tim. 6:16). Man lives his life in the "shadow of death" (Mt.

4:16). One of the apocalyptic riders whom John saw moving across the pages of history had the name Death, and Hades followed him (Rev. 6:8). This rider will continue to do his deadly work until Jesus comes when there shall be no more death (Rev. 21:4). Man fears death; this fear enslaves him (Heb. 2:15).

Death is not viewed as a law of nature or as a biological question in the New Testament. Nor is death over portrayed as a heroic achievement. The death of Christ on the cross is the symbol of abject weakness, by which God's power is manifested. It is said that in early Methodism a person's spirituality was at times measured by the joy with which he greeted death. We won't dispute the claim that the early followers of Wesley "died well," but the Bible does not portray death as a sweet release, but as a fierce monster. Cullmann writes, "The New Testament knows of no optimistic view of death as a 'friend' which frees the soul from the bonds of the body. Such an understanding is excluded by the view of death as the terrible consequence of sin."[2]

It is man's sin that has given death its "sting" (1 Cor. 15:56). "The wages of sin is death," says Paul (Rom. 6:23). Death is seen as God's judgment on man's sin. In the universality of death the universality of man's guilt and his need of redemption become evident. "That man is by nature mortal and therefore subject to death, and that death came into the world through man's sin are two viewpoints expressed in the scripture."[3] The cause of death which the doctor establishes is not, in the thinking of biblical writers, the real cause. Man does not die simply from this or that illness, but because he is a sinner.

If death is the consequence of sin, then the power of death can be broken only if sin is removed. The good news of the gospel is that Christ died "for us," and that he now holds "the keys of Death and Hades" (Rev. 1:18). Hades, the abode of the dead, was thought of as having many doors, since everyone eventually went there. That explains why John portrays Christ as having the keys to every entrance to Hades. Christ by his death and resurrection has "abolished death and brought life and immortality to light through the gospel" (2 Tim. 1:10). Through faith in him there has come a reversal of human destiny: life is no longer a journey into death, but into eternal life.

The writer to the Hebrews says that Christ became man so "that through death he might destroy him who has the power of death, that is, the devil, and deliver all those who through fear of death were subject to lifelong bondage" (2:14, 15). Through his death the fierce enemy of mankind was overcome. Triumphantly the church can sing: "Death is swallowed up in victory. O death, where is thy victory? O death, where is thy sting?" (1 Cor. 15:54 f.). Death met its match on that first Easter morning. Mortality was swallowed up by life and the glory of Easter chased away the dread of the unknown.

Like all gifts of redemption, freedom from the power of death is experienced as a foretaste of our future redemption, but only as long as we are in this mortal existence here on earth. In our earthly body we groan as we wait for the redemption of the body. Sooner or later our earthly tent will be broken down (2 Cor. 5:1); "while we are still in this tent, we sigh with anxiety" (5:4). Our bodies of flesh and blood are not suited for the new mode of existence which awaits us in the world to come, so we long for the day when mortality will "put on immortality" (1 Cor. 15:53).

It is for this reason that Paul can speak of death as "the last enemy" that is to be overcome (1 Cor. 15:26). Not only has Christ freed the believer from the fear of death but physical death itself has been served notice of its demise. The cross has changed the shape of death; instead of a frightening specter, it has now become the pathway of life into the presence of God.

Death is treated realistically by the biblical writers. They do not shy away from using the word death (*thanatos*). There are, however, some interesting metaphors for death in the New Testament which illuminate the Christian's view of death.

Euphemisms for Death

Since death is such a dreadful reality, most languages have

some euphemistic expressions which tend to take the sharp edge
from this subject. The New Testament has several euphemisms as
well. In 2 Corinthians 5 Paul faces the prospect of death. He
recognizes that his body is but a temporary structure, adequate to
shelter him for a few short years of earthly pilgrimage. It is "as
vulnerable to the winds of circumstance and the wear and tear of
everyday life as a 'tabernacle' or tent."[4]

The tent life of the Israelites in the wilderness, com-
memorated annually by the festival of booths, became a biblical
symbol of man's transitory life on earth. Reaching back into Pa-
triarchial times, Abraham's tent life also became a prototype of
the transitory life of the Christian sojourner. However, even secular writers in Paul's day might speak of the fragility of human
existence as life in a tent. Paul knew that unless he survived the
Lord's return, this "tent house" would be broken down. He uses
the picture of breaking up camp, dismantling the tent (*kataluo*; 2
Cor. 5:1).

Another metaphor that he employs for death is "departure"
(*analuo*, Phil. 1:23; *analusis*, 2 Tim. 4:6). This may have a nautical
background, meaning departure from the harbor, lifting the an-
chors. Or it may also be a reference to pulling-up stakes, pulling
up the tent-pegs, in order to leave. In that event there is little differences between the figure of speech in these passages and that
of 2 Corinthians 5:1.

Much more common is the euphemism "sleep." We must, of
course, be careful not to infer from this metaphor that the dead
are unconscious. The believers who die before the return of Christ
are said to "fall asleep through Jesus" (a legitimate translation of
1 Thess. 4:14). As a mother puts her child to bed, so Jesus puts his
own children to sleep—to be raised up at the resurrection. This
was a common Jewish metaphor, as can be seen from the story of
the death of Lazarus (Jn. 11). When Jesus told his disciples that
Lazarus was asleep, they thought it was a sign of his improved
health, and so Jesus had to explain that he meant that Lazarus had
died.

There is another euphemism for death in 1 Corinthians 15:42, 43, where Paul likens death to a seed that falls into the ground, from which a new body springs. "What is sown is perishable, what is raised is imperishable. It is sown in dishonor, it is raised in glory. It is sown in weakness, it is raised in power." This is a very graphic way of speaking of death.

Returning once more to 2 Corinthians 5, Paul may be speaking of death as an undressing (vv. 3, 4). He is not exactly excited at the prospect of being made naked at death, when he must lay aside this earthly dress, his mortal body. He would rather be absorbed immediately into the fuller life of heaven. And with this we have come to the question of the intermediate state.

The Intermediate State

Wrong Views

First of all we must repudiate the Greek doctrine of the immortality of the soul. In Platonic dualism human beings were thought to consist of two parts—a body and soul. The body belonged to this world, the seen (phenomenal) world; the soul belonged to the unseen world. At best the body was a hindrance to the soul. It was a tomb of the soul. At death the soul could finally leave the body and take its flight in the unseen (noumenous) world.[5] It has been said that for the Greek, a human being is an "embodied soul," and for the Hebrew, an "animated body." That may be an oversimplification; nonetheless, the Bible teaches the death and the resurrection of the body, rather than the immortality of the soul.

In popular usage the "immortality of the soul" is not always used in the Greek sense. Rather, it is used to signify simply that man lives forever. But we must be careful not to impose Greek philosophy on biblical language. This Platonic dualism of the mortality of the body and the immortality of the soul not only makes death innocuous; this view also robs evil of its sting, for death cannot touch the eternal soul, and the soul is essentially good in contrast to the body. "The opinion that men are immortal because our soul is of an indestructible, because divine, essence is, once for all, irreconcilable with the biblical view of God and man."[6]

The Bible leaves no doubt about the continuity between our existence here on earth and our existence in the world to come. It does not teach what Plato meant by the immortality of the soul. *I* must die, and *I* will be raised to life, and *I* must stand before God.

Another view which must be questioned is the Roman Catholic doctrine of purgatory. Since the Roman Catholic Church has accepted the Apocrypha as canonical, 2 Maccabees 12:39-45 is used to give biblical legitimacy to this teaching. Once this apocryphal writing is accepted, passages such as 1 Corinthians 3:10-15 and 2 Timothy 1:18 have been interpreted so as to undergird this doctrine. Since all Christians commit venial sin, it is held, there must be a place of purification before one can attain to the beatific vision of God. Souls in purgatory can be helped, so it is taught, by the prayers and other good works of the faithful on earth. However, one can hardly derive such teachings from the New Testament, and so we reject them.

One of the early church leaders who contributed to the idea of purgatory was Tertullian (died ca. AD 230). He taught that when believers died they passed into the "lower world" where they remained until the resurrection. There was one exception, however: the souls of the martyrs went directly to the Lord. At first he thought judgment took place only after the resurrection, but later he held that judgment took place at death. We also find in Tertullian the beginnings of the doctrine of purgatory, for he taught that those who go into the lower world are disciplined in preparation for the resurrection.

The doctrine of the intermediate state raises many questions. We may ask: When does the believer stand before the judgment seat of Christ, at death or after the resurrection? Can there be true blessedness in the intermediate state prior to the final triumph of the kingdom of God? If a believer, when he dies, goes to be with the Lord, what more is there to expect at Christ's coming?

As we turn to the New Testament, we must examine a problem text (2 Cor. 5:1-10).

Away from the Body

Paul is certain that when the earthly tent in which he lives is destroyed, he will acquire a building from God, "a house not made with hands, eternal in the heavens" (v. 1). There may be an allusion here to the stationary temple buildings on Mt. Zion in contrast to the tent life of Israel in the wilderness. The language is reminiscent of Jesus' saying: "I will destroy this temple that is made with hands, and in three days I will build another, not made with hands" (Mk. 14:58). If this passage was in Paul's mind, he may have seen a connection between Christ's resurrection body and ours. However, there is some debate on whether the "building" in heaven is a reference to the resurrection body or the eternal abode which Jesus has prepared for his own (Jn. 14:2).

In any case this heavenly dwelling is not made by human hands. It is not of this creation. This house in the heavens, this shelter made by God, is compared to clothing which Paul would like to put on when he dies (v. 2). The last thing he desires is to be found naked (v. 3).

Paul goes on to say that he does not want to be unclothed. He would much rather be "further clothed, so that what is mortal may be swallowed up by life" (v. 4). Paul seems to wish to be spared the experience of death (being "unclothed"). He wants to be alive when the Lord comes and so be "clothed upon," that is to receive the resurrection body. While he "would rather be away from the body and at home with the Lord" (v. 8), he is of good cheer even as he continues in this mortal body away from the Lord (v. 6). The presence of the Holy Spirit is for him the guarantee that when the time comes his mortality will give way to immortality.

The question is: Does this passage say anything about the intermediate state? That all depends on how one understands "nakedness" (v. 3) and being "away from the body" (v. 8).

First, there are those who hold that our entire life here in our earthly body is a time of "nakedness," for we have not yet been clothed with the eternal dwelling. Those who hold this view see nothing in the passage that would speak of the intermediate state. To this position the question for Paul is not to be with or without a body, but rather that of two different modes of existence—the earthly and the heavenly. This view is difficult to maintain in the light of the fact that Paul seems to think of a point in time when he leaves this body behind.

Second, there is the view that nakedness refers not to existence in this earthly life, but rather to the shame and guilt when the believer stands before God (cf. 1 Jn. 2:28; Rev. 3:17; 16:15). To be found naked before God would mean to be ashamed.[7] It would mean to be caught unawares and unprepared. While there is some truth to this understanding, it does not seem to fit in very well with the rest of Paul's theology. In 1 Thessalonians 5:4 he says the believer, being a child of the day, will not be caught unawares.

Third, there are those who understand the "undressing," which Paul does not look forward to, as referring to death, when he will lay aside his body. If that is so, then the passage (as in the former views) has nothing to say about the intermediate state. It speaks only of death and of the eternal dwelling into which we shall enter.

Fourth, there are many scholars who understand the term nakedness to refer to the intermediate state. After we lay aside this earthly body, and before we receive the resurrection body, we are in a state of "nakedness." Support for this view has at times been sought in John's vision of the souls under the altar (Rev. 6:9). But "souls" is used in Hebraic thought for people (cf. Acts 2:41). Also, such a mind-body dualism would be foreign to Paul's writings.

This state of nakedness, if it refers to the intermediate state, is not defined by Paul. To say that it means disembodied (asomatic) existence does not help much, although that kind of existence cannot be ruled out categorically.

While nothing is said about this state of nakedness, it is still better to be with the Lord than away from him in the present body. Dahl says, "It is for this reason that, even though death is an 'enemy,' it is better to be at home with Christ as naked and disembodied, than to be living in the body without Christ."[8] Ladd agrees with him, and adds: "Apparently he has been given no divine guidance about the state of the dead after death. All he can say is 'nakedness.' "[9]

Professor F.F. Bruce, however, is of the opinion that the resurrection principle is already at work in the believer by the power of the Spirit. Therefore, physical death will not mean a period of disembodiment, but rather the immediate enjoyment of being at home with the Lord. Perhaps he goes too far, however, when he states that at death the believer is given a new body—the spiritual body which Paul speaks of in 1 Corinthians 15. And this spiritual body, Bruce suggests, is the eternal habitation with which the believer desires to be clothed. This change from our mortal body to the new body will take place in a moment, in the twinkling of an eye. And so there will be no period of nakedness (asomatic existence) at all.[10]

Ladd criticizes Bruce's interpretation on the grounds that Paul related the transformation of the earthly body into the spiritual body to the resurrection of the dead at the coming of Christ.[11] Cullmann writes in similar vein: "It would be a distortion of the New Testament conception of time to say: Those who have died in Christ are already living outside time and are already participating in all that the church expects for the end of the world, that is, the resurrection of the body and the putting on of the *soma pneumatikon* [spiritual body] which really depends on the return of Christ to earth and the re-creation of matter itself."[12]

It would seem, then, that Paul thinks of death as a laying aside of this earthly body like clothing, a being stripped naked. He knows, too, that in the end he will be "clothed upon," when he receives a new body. Also, he has an eternal dwelling place in heaven. He does not really say what his existence is like between death and the resurrection. For that we must turn to other passages.

At Home with the Lord

First, we have Christ's promise to the malefactor on the cross: "Truly, I say to you, today you will be with me in Paradise" (Lk. 23:43). This is a brilliant flash of light thrown into the dark "beyond." Because he had expressed faith in Jesus, he was promised fellowship with Christ in the presence of God immediately after death. The Parable of the Rich Man and Lazarus could be brought in here, also, perhaps. It suggests that at death the righteous go to Abraham's bosom—a Jewish term for the state of bliss in the life after death (Lk. 16:19-31). Also, it should be mentioned that when Stephen was stoned to death he saw Christ standing at the right hand of God to cheer him on and to welcome him home (Acts 7:56).

Second, Paul assures us that neither death nor life can "separate us from the love of God in Christ Jesus our Lord" (Rom. 8:38, 39). Believers who die are said to be "in Christ" (1 Thess. 4:16; cf. 1 Cor. 15:18). In other words, the fellowship with Christ which they enjoy by faith here on earth is not broken at death. "If we live, we live to the Lord, and if we die, we die to the Lord; so then, whether we live or whether we die, we are the Lord's" (Rom. 14:8). Death cannot separate us from Christ.

Paul adds one other dimension to this in Philippians 1:21. Facing martyrdom he declares that for him "to die is gain." Life in the flesh is full of troubles, trails, and limitations; death makes an end of earthly sufferings. When he dies, Paul says, he goes to be with Christ and "that is far better" (Phil. 1:23). If we knew nothing more about the intermediate state than this, we could be content. To say that life after death is very much better (a kind of triple comparative) makes all speculation about the intermediate state unnecessary. If it is very much better than life here on earth, what more do we need?

Third, we have the words of assurance which John heard in

one of his apocalyptic visions: " 'Blessed are the dead who die in the Lord henceforth.' 'Blessed indeed,' says the Spirit, 'that they may rest from their labors . . .' " (Rev. 14:13).

Finally, the writer to the Hebrews makes a passing reference "to the spirits of just men made perfect" (Heb. 12:23). The Old Testament saints have found perfection by Christ's sacrifice. Together with the New Testament saints after death, they enjoy fellowship with God. Old Testament saints had an aversion for Sheol, the abode of the dead, because they felt that there was no fellowship with God there. But the witness of writers in the New Testament is that when a believer dies he or she passes on to be with Christ.

Herman Ridderbos sums up the question on life after death in these words:

> The question is whether we are able to say anything more about being with Christ after death than that it is an existence hidden with Christ in heaven, which is one day to be revealed with him. It is to be no longer in the earthly body and therefore freed from all imperfection, sin, and affliction in this body. For that reason it can also be described by Paul as 'gain'. . . . On the other hand, it is not yet to be in the glorified body. . . . [13]

For the believer to know that, should he die before the Lord returns, he will go to be with Christ, be personally with the Lord, see him, be permitted to share his company, live in his presence, while waiting for the resurrection day, is enough to drive the fear of death away. Whether we live when the Lord comes or whether we die in this interim between the cross and the Parousia, we are the Lord's.

> The last end of our hoping is not (as the Buddhist believes) the cessation of all desire and absorption into the divine essence, but an arising from death's sleep into a quite new existence where earth's sorrows and sins will be no more, and in the presence of God and his Christ, with the company of all the redeemed, our personalities will find fulfillment and final blessedness. [14]

Discussion Questions

1. The author indicates that our society tries to avoid the subject of death. What are some of the evidences of this? Are these some signs which indicate a reversal of this tendency to deny death?

2. In the face of death, life takes on a new meaning. Le Comte said, "Death can make even triviality momentous." What do you suppose he meant by that?

3. What is the cause of death from the biblical standpoint? See Romans 6:23; 1 Corinthians 15:56. What change came about in death as a result of Christ's death? Consult 1 Corinthians 15:54; 2 Timothy 1:10; Hebrews 2:14, 15. The author says that the power of God was made manifest in weakness through the death of Christ on the cross. Can you think of examples in your own life where this has been true?

4. Even though the Bible does not avoid the subject of death, it does use some metaphors to describe it. Can you think of some? Check out 1 Corinthians 15:42, 43; 2 Corinthians 5:1-4; Philippians 1:23; 1 Thessalonians 4:14.

5. In brief, what is the difference between the Greek and biblical views of death? What difference does it make how we look at life? Our bodies? The afterlife?

6. What does the Bible have to say about the intermediate state between death and Christ's second coming? Consult Luke 23:43; 16:19-31; Acts 7:55, 56; Romans 8:38, 39; Philippians 1:21, 23; 1 Thessalonians 4:16; Hebrews 12:23. What are some of the lines of interpretation of 2 Corinthians 5:1-10? Is speculation about the intermediate state helpful to the Christian life?

7. Suppose you were to find out that you have only six months to live. How would you change your lifestyle, if at all?

CHAPTER FIVE

"And the Man of Lawlessness Shall Be Revealed"

While the doctrine of Antichrist can hardly be called a central teaching of the New Testament, it looms rather large in the minds of some students of prophecy. Nowhere in the Bible are we exhorted to *wait* for the appearance of Antichrist, as we are to wait for the coming of our Lord. On the other hand, Paul does speak of the *parousia* (the coming) "of the lawless one" (2 Thess. 2:9) at the end of this age, and so we should not evade this dark strand of biblical eschatology.

The term Antichrist is a Christian creation, for until Christ came there could be no Antichrist. ("Anti" originally meant "in the place of." It later came to mean "against.") However, the notion of a sinister figure—the devil's instrument—who opposes God and his Messiah people, is well attested in Jewish sources.

Let us look first at several of these prototypes of the Christian concept of Antichrist.

Prototypes in Jewish History

One of the roots of the Jewish concept of antimessiah is to be found in Gog of Magog (Ezek. 38—39). This figure rises up against God (and in later thought, against Messiah) and his people, and is then utterly destroyed by God. This idea is taken up by John in Revelation 20, where he describes the final onslaught of the forces of evil against God and his people.

Much better known as a prototype of Antichrist, however, is King Antiochus IV (Epiphanes). This Syrian king, portrayed, so it seems, in Daniel 8:23 ff. (see 1 Macc. 1:54, 59), sought to eradicate the Jewish faith. In 168 BC he desecrated the Jerusalem temple by erecting an altar to Zeus over the altar in the court and sacrificing a pig on it. This came to be known as "the abomination that makes desolate" (Dan. 9:27; 11:31; 12:11), for by this despicable pagan outrage the temple was emptied of its worshipers.

The defeat of Antiochus, predicted in Daniel, did not usher in the golden age the Jews were waiting for, and so it was held that this prophecy was as yet unfulfilled (cf. Dan. 11:36, 37). "Accordingly, the Jews still looked for a Man of Sin who should concentrate in himself the powers of evil and whose appearance would be a sign of the last time."[1]

When the Roman general, Pompey, overthrew Jerusalem in 63 BC, he was thought of as continuing that abomination which makes desolate (see Psalms of Solomon ii:1,29; xvii:13). Moreover, the prophecy of Daniel about the "abomination of desolation" was called to mind once again when in AD 40 the Emperor Gaius (Caligula) ordered that an image of himself be set up in the Jerusalem temple (Josephus, *Jewish Antiquities*, XIX, i.1).

While this catastrophe was averted by the death of Gaius, the temple was destroyed (and desecrated) by Titus in AD 70. Again Josephus sees in that debacle a fulfillment of Daniel's prediction of the "abomination of desolation" (*Antiquities* X.xi.7). (In Mark's Gospel Jesus predicts the destruction of Jerusalem and counsels his followers to flee to the mountains when they see "the desolating sacrilege set up where it ought not to be," 13:14.)

In IV Ezra 11—12, (2 Esdras) written in the first century AD, the Roman oppressors of the Jews are symbolized by an eagle. A lion, symbolizing the Messiah, condemns the eagle for its tyranny and the eagle is destroyed. It is not hard to see why the eagle, symbolizing the oppressive Roman overlord, should be thought of by the Jews as the epitome of all wickedness, and as antimessiah. Nor is it hard to imagine how Nero came to be thought of as antimessiah (Sib. Oracles 5:93-110). It was he, according to rumor, who had escaped across the Euphrates, to return some day with Eastern hordes to devastate the empire and sack Jerusalem.

Needless to say, the idea of sinister personages, who oppose God and his people, was close at hand when the New Testament was written. The Jewish concept of an antigod or antimessiah was transposed, under the guidance of the Spirit, into the Christian doctrine of Antichrist.

Antichrists and the Present Age

For the Christian doctrine of Antichrist we must turn to the New Testament. The term "antichrist" is found only five times, and in John's letters alone (1 Jn. 2:18, 22; 4:3; 2 Jn. 7). The concept of Antichrist, however, is found also in several other passages of the New Testament. It is of significance that both the singular and the plural are used when speaking of antichrist. There are antichrists who oppose God and his people throughout this age, and there is an Antichrist who emerges at the end of the age.

What do the New Testament writers have to say about the forerunners of the Antichrist who is to appear in the end?

In Mark 13 our Lord predicts there will be many false christs—not just one—and many false prophets (Mk. 13:21-23). These false christs will perform signs and wonders and will deceive and lead people astray. In the immediate context this seems to be a reference primarily to the numerous abortive pseudo-messianic rebellions that preceded and followed AD 70. However, in the wider context of the chapter, this is a warning to Christians living in the end-times not to be deceived by pseudochrists.

Quite in line with Jesus' prediction is Paul's explanation that before our Lord returns there will be a falling away, the rebellion. Then the man of lawlessness will be revealed (2 Thess. 2:3). Whereas he had not yet appeared in Paul's day, "the mystery of lawlessness" was already at work (2 Thess. 2:7). Just as there are mysteries in God's plan of salvation, so there are also secrets in sin.

Man cannot comprehend God's saving purposes by his own contemplation, and he needs the illumination of God's Spirit also to fathom the depths of iniquity. Many of the evils of our society are blamed on economics, political structures, heredity, or environment. And while these play a part in creating the malaise with which all human life is infected, secular man doesn't have the eyes to see that behind these forces there is a demonic power at work.

The same theme is struck by the Apostle John in his first and second epistles. The evidence for the conviction that the last hour has begun, says John, is that Antichrist comes, indeed many antichrists have already come into existence (1 Jn. 2:18). John does not name them. But he points out that "the spirit of Antichrist" (1 Jn. 4:3), who will come in the end, is already at work in his forerunners.

What kind of work do they do? Among other things they deny that Jesus is the Christ (1 Jn. 2:22). Whoever does that is the liar *par excellence,* inspired by Antichrist—not the personal Antichrist who is still to come, but a living embodiment of his demonic spirit (1 Jn. 4:3; 2 Jn. 7). Anyone who denies the truth is a very antichrist, "just as we might speak of a supremely evil person as 'the very devil.' "[2]

This double vision of the activity of antichrists in the present, and of Antichrist at the end of the age, is also reflected in the Revelation. Here this sinister personage is portrayed as the Beast. Indeed, John has a vision of two beasts, one from the sea and one from the land (Rev. 13). The first beast has ten horns and seven heads, and has a mortal wound that is healed. No doubt the four great beasts of Daniel 7:3 suggested this monster to John. The mortal wound that healed is probably a reference to the death of Nero. It gets its authority from the Dragon (Satan), and men worship both the Beast and the Dragon.

In John's day this Beast symbolized the autocratic rule of Rome with its caesar cult, which led to the violent oppression of the Christian church. The blasphemous names on the seven heads of the Beast reflect the increasing tendency of the Roman emperors to assume titles of deity. The hope that the beast might die soon (it had a mortal wound) proved illusory (it healed). Similarly in John's day, and in every generation since, this beast does its deadly work, inspired by Satan.

The second beast has two horns like a lamb, but speaks like a dragon. It performs miracles and deceives people. Above all, as the first beast's "right-hand man" it enforces worship of the first beast. While ostensibly appearing as a Christlike lamb, it is actually Satanic in character. It is a pseudochrist.

These two beasts appeared in John's day as Roman caesar and the caesar cult—with politics and religion intricately interwoven. They raise armies for the final conflict, which is to occur when Christ returns with his heavenly armies (Rev. 19). Finally, Antichrist (the first beast) and his false prophet (the second beast) are cast into the lake of fire.

Quite clearly, then, the apostles teach that while satanic personages, antichrists, and pseudochrists may emerge throughout the present age, all these evil powers will find their epitome in the Antichrist at the end of this age.

Antichrist and the Coming of Christ

Daniel's prophecy of "the abomination that makes desolate," which was partly fulfilled when Antiochus Epiphanes desecrated the temple in 168 BC, was not thought to have been finally fulfilled. Nor was it completely fulfilled in the destruction of the temple in AD 70, for which event Jesus had used Daniel's phrase (Mk. 13:14; Lk. 21:20, 21). Paul taught that preceding the End there would be a further outbreak of evil sacrilege, the principle of which was already at work in the history of humankind. We turn then to 2 Thessalonians 2:1-12 to see what Paul has to say about this eschatological figure who is to be the embodiment of evil prior to Christ's return.

The church at Thessalonica was stirred up by the notion that

Christ's return was to take place any moment. To calm the troubled waters Paul explains that the "day will not come, unless the rebellion comes first, and the man of lawlessness is revealed, the son of perdition, who opposes and exalts himself against every so-called god or object of worship, so that he takes his seat in the temple of God, proclaiming himself to be God" (2 Thess. 2:3, 4).

This champion of wickedness cannot simply be identified with one of the many prototypes and forerunners of Antichrist, for our passage makes it plain that he is someone who comes upon the scene at the end of this age. Leon Morris says: "The Man of Lawlessness is an eschatological personage. Paul wrote that he will appear just before the Lord comes again. Accordingly it is futile to try to identify him."[3]

This "man of sin" (as an alternate reading has it) will be "revealed" (vv. 3, 8); that is, he exists in the world prior to his manifestation at the end of history. For this reason he is said to have a *parousia* (v. 9)—a word that describes also our Lord's glorious appearing at his second advent.

The description of the diabolical designs of this evil monster includes a reference to his sitting in God's temple and proclaiming that he is God (v. 4). Some are of the opinion that Paul has the Jerusalem temple in mind which, in that event, would have to be rebuilt. But the apostles of the New Testament speak only of the demise of the temple in Jerusalem, never of its reconstruction in the end times. Others recognize that the church is now God's temple, and that Ezekiel's prophecy of a new temple was fulfilled in the church. Thus, they suggest that Antichrist will do his destructive work in the church ("sitting in the temple of God"). However, while the apostles do know of a falling away in the last days, they do not expect the true church to become apostate. Moreover, John in his first Epistle explains that antichrists had already come in his day, leading some to forsake the faith (1 Jn. 2:18, 19).

In the light of the long history of temple defilements, beginning with Antiochus Epiphanes and ending with the destruction of the temple by Titus in AD 70, it would appear that Paul is simply using traditional language ("the abomination that desolates" the temple) to describe Antichrist's subtle and sinister attacks upon God, his people, and all that is holy.

During this interim—between Christ's first and second coming—"the mystery of lawlessness" is at work, but the final revelation of the power of evil is being restrained (vv. 6, 7). This is a sign of God's patience with mankind, for he wants all to come to the knowledge of the truth. Paul's readers no doubt knew who or what this restraining power was. We do not. Many suggestions have been made, but none of them is entirely convincing.

One popular view is that Paul thought of Rome with its law and order as that which restrained evil. Since the Roman state has disappeared, this view has been extended to include government *per se*, by which the forces of evil are restrained. Unfortunately some governments function more like the Beast of Revelation 13, than the servant of God (Rom. 13:4).

Oscar Cullmann has suggested that the preaching of the gospel is the restraining power. Since Paul speaks of "that which restrains" (neuter) and "him who restrains" (masculine), Moore (following Cullmann) suggests that Paul thought of himself (as preacher of the gospel) as the one who restrains. That the gospel shall be preached in all the world before the end comes is clearly taught by Jesus (Mk. 13:10); but it would be extremely extraordinary if Paul should have thought that he was keeping Antichrist from being revealed.

Many hold that the Holy Spirit is the restraining power (and Person). By convicting man of sin and drawing him to Christ through the gospel, the Spirit restrains the development of evil. The problem with this view is that when God's hour strikes, this restrainer is to be put out of the way (v. 7). That could hardly be said of the Holy Spirit.

Others have suggested that the restrainer is some angelic being (say Michael) who serves as a check on the growing power of sin. Professor George Ladd holds that God himself is the

Restrainer. He must then, however, change the final clause of verse 7 to read: "Until he (i.e. Antichrist) come out of the midst"—a strained rendering of the text, to say the least.[5]

Perhaps we need not be specific at all. We should be thankful that in God's providence the demonic power of evil is being kept in check, making it possible for the church to complete its mission. However, when this day of salvation is over, then the demonic power of evil will be fully manifested and find its representation in some incredibly godless personage.

Since leaders who appear to be the very embodiment of wickedness, come on the scene of history from time to time, Bible students have frequently succumbed to the temptation to identify some historical personage as Antichrist. To show how misdirected such attempts often are, let us look at some of these identifications.

Identifications of Antichrist

In the Revelation, John sees a forerunner of Antichrist in the Roman totalitarian power. The Roman state demanded ultimate loyalty of its subjects, persecuting the people of God who confess Christ as Lord, rather than Caesar. This cruel monster (the Beast) was raging in John's day, and was seen as the leader of all powers arraigned against God at the end of the age.

It was quite natural, therefore, for some writers in the early Christian centuries to identify those Roman rulers who oppressed the church as Antichrist. Some of them were paragons of iniquity: Nero, Domitian, Diocletian, and Julian the Apostate are examples. When Islam threatened to overwhelm the Eastern Church, however, Muhammad was identified as Antichrist. His name was slightly changed to make it yield the approximate number, 666.

In Western Christendom, on the other hand, whisperings that the pope might be the Antichrist were heard (although the Roman pope, Gregory I, applied that sinister title to the patriarch of the Eastern Church). Throughout the Middle Ages, however, there appeared to be good reason for people to believe that the

Roman pontiff and his ilk might possibly be the fulfillment of
Paul's prophecy of the coming man of sin. John Wycliffe in the
last year of his life (1384) wrote a treatise in which he gave twelve
reasons for holding that the pope was indeed the Antichrist.

This identification continued into the Reformation, and
some of the Reformation churches incorporated this view in their
confessions of faith. The translators of the King James Version
(1611) complimented the king for giving the man of sin (the pope)
a mortal blow by authorizing this version. For about 200 years
after the Reformation the prevailing view of Protestant exegetes
was that the pope was the Antichrist. The godly Matthew Henry,
of commentary fame, was so convinced that the Roman Church
was the Babylonian whore of the Revelation, that he called on
Christians to share actively in military measures against the papal
Antichrist.[6] Some of the Anabaptist leaders, however, felt that the
notorious title "Antichrist" could just as well be applied to the
Protestant state churches who persecuted them, winked at gross
evils, and joined hands with the secular powers.

While a corrupt and powerful church (Roman or Protestant)
may have appeared like the Beast at times, as did the Rome of the
Caesars in John's day, these interpretations tended to overlook the
fact that Paul had an eschatological personage in mind. Therefore, to identify a certain pope as Antichrist was tantamount to
saying that Christ's advent was just around the corner which, of
course, some did say.

Toward the end of the 18th century the pietistic writer Jung-
Stilling became convinced that Antichrist was at hand. He saw
this in the political developments and in the spiritual decline of
the church. In order to seek refuge during the tribulation that was
imminent, he encouraged an exodus of believers to Asia, where
the whole endeavor came to naught.

Edward Irving (1792-1834) taught that the 1,260 years during
which the Beast of Revelation does its devastating work covered
the period from AD 533 to 1793. AD 533 was the year the emperor Justinian gave the bishop of Rome authority over the

churches, acknowledging the pope as head of the church; AD 1793 was when the French Revolution broke out. This he explained was the judgment on Babylon (Rome), and he suggested consequently that the final battle (Armageddon) would occur in 1868.[7]

More recently, when the Roman Catholic, John F. Kennedy, became president of the United States, many Protestants thought the end of this age was near, particularly when he was wounded in the head by an assassin's bullet. Even after his death some expected him to rise from his coffin and be revealed as Antichrist.

But before Kennedy, Hitler and Stalin seemed to fit the descriptions of this man of sin quite well. Albert Einstein received a letter from a prophecy student informing him that Mussolini was the Antichrist and that Einstein was the false prophet.

When it was noticed by some student of this subject that the wicked king in Daniel 11:21 (the prototype of Antichrist) was to gain his kingdom by flattery, Henry Kissinger got into the picture, since he masterminded detente. From time to time it had been suggested by Bible readers that Antichrist would be a Jew who disregarded the God of his fathers (Dan. 11:37). That seemed to fit Kissinger perfectly. Another Jew who has denied the God of his fathers, and who has a wound that is healed (a lost eye), is Moshe Dayan. Some have picked him as candidate for the office of Antichrist. (Interestingly, such identifications are often made by people who believe that the church will be with the Lord when Antichrist emerges.)[8]

All such speculations lead us nowhere. We are not instructed to look for the appearing of Antichrist, but for the appearing of our Lord and Savior Jesus Christ. For all we know, Antichrist may be strutting on the stage of history at this moment, ready to be revealed.

What we do know for certain is this: when Antichrist will be revealed, "the Lord Jesus will slay him with the breath of his mouth and destroy him by his appearing and his coming" (the *epiphaneia* of his *parousia*, 2 Thess. 2:8). Then all those who have suffered under this Beast will reign with Christ.

In the dispensational system of interpreting the Bible, it is taught that Antichrist will emerge only after the rapture. (I am told that books are now available informing people who will be left behind at Christ's return how they can circumvent the wiles of Antichrist and so slip into the millennium where under the evangelization efforts of converted Jews they will be saved.) But 2 Thessalonians 2:1-12 makes it explicitly clear that Antichrist will be revealed before the coming of Christ. For this reason the church needs to be prepared at all times to suffer persecution, as it always has in some parts of the world.

There is still much blithe optimism around that steadfastly proclaims that the world is getting better and better. The doctrine of Antichrist is a reminder to us to take seriously the power of sin and Satan in human history. Without God's armor (Eph. 6) even the believers are sure to be outwitted and overcome. Is it not ironical that an age which looks on the doctrines of devil and Antichrist as remnants of beliefs from the dark ages, is now witnessing the most appalling manifestations of demonic statecraft? Think only of the invasion of the occult, the proliferation of false cults, the gruesome crimes, the terrible cruelties that have characterized this enlightened century.

Paul Althaus affirms that the concept of Antichrist is God's loud "No!" to the optimistic faith in the idea that God's kingdom will progressively come here on earth, (brought about by human effort)[9]. Emil Brunner makes the observation that "the two symbols, that of the millennium and that of Antichrist, stand over against each other in mutual limitation. Neither an optimistic nor a pessimistic view of history is permitted us."[10] If the doctrine of the millennium reflects the bright line in human history, then the doctrine of Antichrist reflects the dark underground force operative throughout history until God ushers in the heavenly state.

We have the assurance that the One in us is stronger than the one who is in the world. No matter how great the power of evil, it cannot overcome the power of God. With that assurance we want to help the needy, lift the fallen, and proclaim the good news while it is day. Night comes when no man can work.

Discussion Questions

1. What is the difference between false christs (antichrists) and the eschatological figure called Antichrist? The relevant texts are 1 John 2:18, 22; 4:3; 2 John 7; Mark 13:21-23; 2 Thessalonians 2:1-12; Revelation 13. What are some of the characteristics of antichrists?

2. Who were some of the prototypes of Antichrist in Jewish history? What did King Antiochus IV (Epiphanes) do to merit the attention of Daniel? See Daniel 8:23 ff.; 9:27; 11:31; 12:11. What is meant by "the abomination of desolation" used both by Daniel and Jesus (Mk. 13:14)?

3. The author says that "just as there are mysteries in God's plan of salvation, so there are also secrets in sin." What does he mean by this? How and why is sin more visible to the eyes of faith than to unfaith?

4. What are some of the explanations for the power which restrains the man of lawlessness (2 Thess. 2:6, 7)? Which explanation seems most plausible to you? Why? When will the man of lawlessness no longer be restrained?

5. Numerous figures have been identified as the Antichrist throughout church history. Who did the Antichrist stand for in John's Revelation? What figure was identified with Antichrist during and after the Reformation? What figures in the twentieth century received this appellation? Why? Why are such associations misguided?

6. Though it is risky to identify persons with Antichrist, the spirit of Antichrist is present in every age. Where in our society is this demonic spirit present? Why is it unnecessary for the Christian to despair in the face of this evil? Note the comfort given in 1 John 4:4.

CHAPTER SIX

"Behold He Comes with the Clouds"

The chaotic movements of history, with all their ups and downs, will finally fall into place when God ushers in the end. Despite appearances, history is not "a tale told by an idiot, full of sound and fury, signifying nothing." The day is coming when history will reach its goal. This we know on the authority of God's Word, and so we can labor for him during this interim, knowing that our labors are not in vain in the Lord.

When Christ comes he will complete the plan which God had from the ages. That reign of God which Jesus announced at his first coming will be finally and totally established. In this age we continue to pray that God's kingdom might come. We suffer and sacrifice for the kingdom, and proclaim the good news of the kingdom. But we know that only at the return of our Lord will God's kingdom finally be realized.

This great event for which the church is waiting is described in different ways in the New Testament and is given a great variety of names. While the New Testament does not use the phrase "the return of Christ," it has become one of the more popular ways of identifying Christ's coming at the end of this age. Jesus did of course say that he would come again and take us to himself (Jn. 14:3). Another term which has become part of Christian vocubulary is "the second coming of Christ." Again this phrase is not found in the New Testament, although Hebrews comes close to it when it says, "Christ ... will appear a second time ... to save those who are eagerly waiting for him" (9:29).

Of course, when we speak of Christ's return or of his second coming we do not mean that he is entirely absent during this time of waiting. He promised, before he returned to the Father, that he would be with us "to the close of the age" (Mt. 28:20). He explained that if he did not go away, then the Paraclete could not come to us. Later, when the Spirit was poured out at Pentecost, Christ came to us by his Spirit. But the Holy Spirit is but a down payment, a foretaste, of that which is yet to come (Eph. 1:13, 14).

Another very popular expression (in some evangelical circles) which is not found in the New Testament is "the rapture." Paul does speak in one instance of the church being "caught up" to meet the Lord in the air (1 Thess. 4:17). Our English word rapture comes to us through the Latin Vulgate which in this passage has the Latin *rapiemur* for the Greek *harpagesometha*—to be snatched or caught up.

Whereas several of these popular ways of speaking of the coming of Christ at the end of the age are not exact translations of any biblical word or phrase, they are, of course, perfectly legitimate ways of speaking of this great eschatological event. We need to ask, however, what key biblical terms are used of Christ's coming. What are the names for this glorious day at the end of history? How is this event described? What is its significance for us? These and other questions shall concern us in this chapter.

The Vocabulary for the Coming of Christ
The Day

The great event for which the church is waiting is often called simply "the day." Jesus said, "On that day many will say to me, 'Lord, Lord' ..." (Mt. 7:22). Paul writes, "But you are not in darkness, brethren, for that day to surprise you like a thief" (1 Thess. 5:4). Again, "Each man's work will become manifest; for the Day will disclose it" (1 Cor. 3:13). Of Onesiphorus Paul says,

"May the Lord grant him to find mercy from the Lord on that Day" (2 Tim. 1:18; cf. 2 Tim. 1:12). The writer to the Hebrews exhorts his readers not to neglect meeting together but rather to encourage one another, "all the more as you see the Day drawing near" (10:25). The term "day" has its background in the Old Testament, where *ha yom* (the day) points forward to God's final act in history (e.g. Mal. 3:17).

Also, this day is called "the great day" (Jude 6; Rev. 6:17; 16:14). And, of course, it is the "last day" (Jn. 6:39, 40, 44). It is a day of judgment for the wicked (Rom. 2:5; Mt. 11:22; 1 Jn. 4:17; 2 Pet. 2:9). But it is also a day of deliverance for the saints (Eph. 4:30). Peter writes that the believers are being guarded by God's power for "salvation ready to be revealed in the last time" (1 Pet. 1:5; "time" here is the equivalent of "day").

Most significantly this day is called "the day of the Lord" (1 Thess. 5:2; 2 Thess. 2:2), or, in an expanded form, "the day of our Lord Jesus Christ" (1 Cor. 1:8; 5:5), or simply "the day of Jesus Christ" or "Christ" (Phil. 1:6; 2:16). (The "day of God" occurs twice in the New Testament, 2 Pet. 3:12; Rev. 16:14.) The background for the concept of the "day of the Lord" (and its variants) is to be found in the Old Testament (cf. Amos 5:18-20). In the Old Testament it is made plain that the day of the Lord (the *yom Yahweh*) will be a terrible day for the godless, but a day of salvation for the righteous (Mal. 3:2; 4:1, 5).

The Coming

This great day at the end of time is the day of Christ's "coming." This term also has its Old Testament counterpart in the coming of Yahweh, who as the living God performs mighty deeds in the history of humankind. Jesus predicted that he, the Son of man, would come (*erchomai*) "on the clouds of heaven" (Mt. 24:30; Mk. 13:26; Lk. 21:27). The day and the hour of his coming are not known, however (Mk. 13:32; Mt. 24:36; Acts 1:7). The believer is to watch. Christ will come like a thief in the night (Mt. 24:42 f.; 1 Thess. 5:2), although those who belong to the light will not be caught by surprise. One conviction pervades the New Testament and that is that Christ will come soon. "Surely I am coming soon," John hears Christ saying (Rev. 22:20). And during Christ's absence the church continues to pray Maranatha, "Lord, Come!" (1 Cor. 16:22); it proclaims his death "until he comes" (1 Cor. 11:26).

The Parousia

This coming of Christ for which the church waits is called the *parousia* in the New Testament. In classical Greek that word meant simply the arrival or presence of persons or things. Indeed it is still used in that nonreligious sense in several places in the New Testament. For example, Paul rejoices at the *parousia* of Stephanas (1 Cor. 16:17). He is comforted by the *parousia* of Titus (2 Cor. 7:6). He speaks of his own *parousia* (Phil. 2:12).

However, the word was used also as a technical term to describe the arrival of the emperor or some dignitary for an official visit.[1] These visits (*parousiai*) of rulers were always celebrated with great pomp and circumstance. Cities were cleaned and roads were repaired in anticipation of the king's *parousia*, and coins were minted to celebrate the great event. Hadrian's travels, for example, can be followed by the coins which were struck to commemorate his visits. One papyrus reads: "Let us labor night and day [to get the town in shape] for the *parousia* of the emperor is near." These words could easily be transposed into a Christian exhortation. (From all appearances it seems as if the word has been sufficiently anglicized so that we no longer use it as a foreign word.) The Latin equivalent of the Greek *parousia* is *adventus*, and so we speak of Christ's first and second Advent—a term not uncommon among Christians.

The New Testament writers use this political term to speak of Christ's arrival at the end of this age. It is also used once of the coming of Antichrist, in 2 Thessalonians 2:9. The gospels use *parousia* rarely (only four times in Matthew), as do some other writers (once in John, twice in James, thrice in Peter), but Paul uses Parousia very frequently (some 14 times).

Perhaps the best-known passages in which Parousia designates Christ's return are to be found in the Thessalonian letters. With great joy Paul anticipates the presence of his converts at the Parousia of the Lord Jesus (1 Thessalonians 2:19, 20). He prays that the hearts of his readers be established in holiness in anticipation of the Parousia of Jesus Christ (1 Thess. 3:13; 5:23). He comforts the bereaved by assuring them that their loved ones who are in Christ will not miss the Parousia (1 Thess. 4:15). But he also warns them against those who stir the churches up by saying that the Parousia has already taken place (2 Thess. 2:1, 2).

The Epiphany

The glorious arrival of the heavenly Imperator at the end of history is known also as his "appearing" or his "manifestation." The Greek word *epiphaneia* (English "epiphany") means literally "to shine upon," and is used of the light that comes from the sun, moon, and stars (Acts 27:20). As a technical religious term it has reference to "a visible manifestation of a hidden divinity, either in the form of a personal appearance or by some deed of power by which its presence is known."[2]

The word is used to describe Christ's first Advent, when God's grace, kindness, and philanthropy "appeared" (Tit. 2:11; 3:4—here the verb form). Through his Advent death was abolished and life and immortality came to light through the gospel (2 Tim. 1:10—here the noun).

In the other passages where the word *epiphaneia* occurs, it refers to Christ's glorious appearing at the end of history. Timothy is challenged to do his work in the light of "the appearing of our Lord Jesus Christ" (1 Tim. 6:14; 2 Tim. 4:1). Paul promises that the Lord will reward him and "all who have loved his appearing" (2 Tim. 4:8). He explains that God's saving grace, which appeared at the first Advent, trains us to deny evil and to wait for "our blessed hope, the appearing of the glory of our great God and Savior Jesus Christ" (Tit. 2:11-13).

To speak of Christ's return as an "appearing" suggests that today he is hidden from our sight. And indeed he is: "Though you do not now see him you believe in him," says Peter (1 Pet. 1:8). He is visible, of course, to the eyes of faith. But one day he will break out of his present hiddenness and "when he appears [*phaneroo*] we shall be like him, for we shall see him as he is" (1 Jn. 3:2).

The Revelation

Closely related to the term Epiphany is the word "revelation" (*apokalupsis*). While the word is used in a variety of ways in the New Testament, it is sometimes employed by the apostles to describe the great day at the end of the age. The Corinthians are said to be waiting "for the revealing of our Lord Jesus Christ" (1 Cor. 1:7). Jesus, says Paul, will be "revealed from heaven with his mighty angels" (2 Thess. 1:7).

The suffering saints will be honored "at the revelation of Jesus Christ" (1 Pet. 1:7, 13; 4:13). Salvation, in its final aspect, will "be revealed in the last time" (1 Pet. 1:5), as will Christ's glory (1 Pet. 5:1; Rom. 8:18).

About the year 1830, it occurred to John Darby that Christ's coming was to take place in two stages, with the "rapture" preceding Christ's coming in glory by some seven years. This was not espoused in the Christian church for 1,800 years, but it has become very popular among evangelical Christians. (Darby, was an early Phymouth Brethren leader in Britain. In Europe they are better known as Darbyists.) The first stage of the Parousia, according to Darby, was to be Christ's coming *for* his saints, whereas the second phase was to be his coming *with* the saints. Between these two comings Darby slipped in seven years of tribulation—a concept borrowed from Daniel. This view is hard to sustain in the light of 2 Thessalonians 1:6, 7, where the suffering of the saints continues right up to Christ's coming in glory; and 2 Thessalonians 2:8, where Antichrist is liquidated at Christ's Parousia.

Alexander Reese writes:

> About 1830, however, a new school arose within the fold of pre-millennialism that sought to overthrow what, since the Apostlic Age, have been considered by all pre-millennialists as established results, and to institute in their place a series of doctrines that had never been heard of before. The school . . . is founded by J. N. Darby.[3]

This scheme of interpretation has many other facets which do not concern us at the moment, but it has led to considerable confusion and division in the ranks of evangelicals regarding the Parousia. If one takes seriously the contexts in which the different terms used for the coming of Christ are found, it seems very arbitrary to make them refer to different "comings." Professor Ladd is correct when he says: "Certainly if one can make anything of language at all, no distinction can be made between the parousia, the apocalypse and the epiphany of our Lord. They are one and the same event."[4]

Having looked at some of the key words used by the biblical writers to refer to the glorious day of Christ's return, we now turn to some brief descriptions of this great event at the end of history. We limit ourselves to three pictures; one from Jesus, another from Paul, and, finally, one from John.

Descriptions of the Coming of Christ
In the Sayings of Jesus

Jesus said that he, the Son of man, would come "in the glory of his Father with the holy angels" (Mk. 8:38). Similarly, in his farewell discourse in Mark 13 (parallels in Matthew 24 and Luke 21), Jesus describes the break-up of this present order with vivid apocalyptic imagery. Then he says: "They will see the Son of man coming in the clouds with great power and glory" (Mk. 13:26, cf. 14:62). He adds that at this appearance he will send forth his angels to gather together his own (v. 27).

Christ's triumphant coming is described in terms of the enthronement of the mysterious figure ("like a son of man") in Daniel 7:13 f. The cloud is a common Old Testament symbol of God's hiddenness, as well as of his revelation. Since this is theological language, and not the vocabulary of astrophysics, we do not need to ask whether the clouds with which Christ returns will be over China or the United States. The cloud not only attended God's revelation in the Old Testament, but it became part of the imagery describing the future day of the Lord (Ezek. 30:3; Joel 2:2). These clouds are chariots of God's glory, which in a unique way embody the divine majesty and power.

"His coming 'with the clouds' will make an end of the veil-edness that characterizes both Jesus and the people of God."[5] As the cloud enveloped our Lord when he ascended into heaven, so he comes with the cloud when he returns in glory (Rev. 1:7).

And when he comes he will send his angels to gather the elect (believers) from "the ends of the earth to the ends of heaven." This terminology represents a synthesis of two Old Testament expressions and means "from everywhere." Words which were used in the Old Testament to express the hope of the gathering of the scattered tribes of Israel are here transmuted and applied to the great gathering of the saints when Jesus comes.

Christ's coming will be a triumphant, glorious, public event. "For as the lightning comes from the east and shines as far as the west, so will be the coming of the Son of man" (Mt. 24:27).

In the Writings of Paul

In the writings of Paul the most vivid descriptions of the return of Christ are to be found in the Thessalonian letters. In 1 Thessalonians 4:16 Paul writes: "For the Lord himself will descend from heaven with a cry of command, with the arch-angel's call, and with the sound of the trumpet of God." The believers, both the living and dead in Christ, shall be caught up together "in the clouds to meet the Lord in the air" (v. 17).

The shouted command is a military word. Paul doesn't say who gives the command. Is it God giving the command that Christ shall return to earth? Is it Christ commanding the dead to rise? Or is it the heavenly Imperator, Jesus Christ, giving the armies of heaven the command to begin to move for the final triumph? What is important is that God and not man determines the end of history.

In Paul's day every parousia of the emperor was signaled by the playing of martial music, the blowing of the trumpet. But of course the trumpet is more than a military metaphor. Already in the Old Testament the trumpet was connected with the great theophanies of God (Ex. 19:17-19). Above all, the trumpet came to be associated with the coming Day of the Lord. "Blow the trumpet in Zion . . . for the day of the Lord is coming" (Joel 2:1). In Matthew 24:31 both trumpet and angels are associated with the ingathering of the elect at the end of the age. Similarly, Paul mentions not only the shouted command and the trumpet (1 Thess. 4:16), but also the voice of the archangel—a reference to that heavenly world which takes such an active part in the great events of redemption history. Those who hold to a "secret" rapture have some difficulty harmonizing that view with such a "loud" and public event.

At this coming of Christ, says Paul, the saints will be caught up together for a meeting in the air with the Lord (1 Thess. 4:17). The word "meeting" (*apantesis*) is another technical term for the reception which was afforded a royal personage when he visited a city. A delegation from the city might go out to meet him and to accompany him into the city along streets lined with people wearing white garments. The word is used, for instance, for the meeting of the Roman brothers with Paul (Acts 28:15; cf. also Mt. 25:6; 27:32). In a religious and technical sense it is found only once in the New Testament, namely in 1 Thessalonians 4:17. Here it refers to the glorious meeting between Christ and his own.[6]

The coming of Christ brings salvation to the saints and judgment to the unbelievers. This double aspect of Yahweh's day is well known from the Old Testament. And so in 2 Thessalonians 1:7-8, Paul describes "When the Lord Jesus is revealed from heaven with his mighty angels in flaming fire, inflicting vengenance upon those who do not know God and upon those who do not obey the gospel of our Lord Jesus." Not only does his coming bring judgment upon those who have rejected Christ, but the leader of the forces of evil will also be punished. "Then the lawless one will be revealed, and the Lord Jesus will slay him with the breath of his mouth and destroy him by his appearing and his coming" (2 Thess. 2:8). In the same passage it is stated that the saints will be given rest when the Lord Jesus is revealed from heaven (v. 7).

In the Visions of John

Other writers of New Testament books also contribute their descriptions of Christ's second coming, but perhaps one more example will suffice. In the last book of the Bible John takes his readers with him into the heavenly world again and again to give them visions of heaven in order to strengthen them in their trials. In chapter seven he has a vision of all the saints coming home to glory. Several times he describes the dissolution of this universe and the final battle that will signal the end of this age. Once this final struggle between God and the forces of evil is called Armageddon (16:16), since all the great battles in Israel's history were fought in the valley of Megiddo.

Finally, after the downfall of the Babylons of this world, and the invitation to all the saints to attend the marriage supper of the Lamb (19:7), John sees the heavens opened and a rider on a white horse appears followed by the armies of heaven (v. 11). According to Rissi, "Present-day interpretation of the Revelation of John is on the whole in agreement that Revelation 19:11-16 describes the return of Jesus Christ."[7] Mounce writes: "The Seer is not describing the gradual conquest of evil in the spiritual struggles of the faithful, but a great historic event which brings to an end the Antichrist and his forces, and ushers in the long-awaited era of righteousness."[8]

That the rider on the white horse is Christ can easily be discerned from the description of this glorious personage. His robe is dipped in blood, and he carries the name, "King of kings and

Lord of lords." The saints "arrayed in fine linen, white and pure, followed him on white horses." The battle is not described, for the judgment against the wicked hosts, led by the Beast (Satan's protege), is carried out by the word which comes from Christ's mouth. The Beast and his false prophet are captured and thrown into the lake of fire; Christ's enemies are slain, and Satan is bound for a thousand years.

We have noticed the great diversity used in the vocabulary and imagery, to describe the return of our Lord. Some of it is borrowed from the Old Testament, some from Jewish apocalyptic, some from the political world in which the writers lived, or from ordinary life. All of it, however, has been employed by the biblical writers, under the inspiration of the Spirit, to portray the triumph of our Lord at the end of the age.

The Parousia is at the very heart of New Testament eschatology. All the aspects of the doctrine of future things is overshadowed by the expectation of the coming of the Savior, Jesus Christ. End-time events are not in focus, but rather the Person of Jesus Christ.

Richard Longenecker writes, "It is the return of Christ, therefore, that is the focus of the futuristic message of the New Testament. Any attempt to shift this focus, whether in theory or in practice and for whatever reasons, can rightly be called 'sectarian' because it alters the thrust of the biblical proclamation."[9] As the chapters of this book indicate, there are various themes of New Testament eschatology which make up the mosaic of scriptural teaching on the last things. However, the return of Christ is not simply one of a dozen other themes in this area of biblical teaching; it is the very heart and center of our hope.

The Parousia has always been a source of great comfort to those who lost loved ones, for they will not be at a disadvantage when Christ comes for his own (1 Thess. 4:15). It has been a great encouragement for God's servants as they labor in Christ's kingdom, as Paul himself found it (1 Thess. 2:19, 20). Also, it has always been an inspiration to live a holy life. Paul writes in his benediction at the end of his first letter to the Thessalonians: "May the God of peace himself sanctify you wholly; and may your spirit and soul and body be kept sound and blameless at the coming of our Lord Jesus Christ" (1 Thess. 5:23).

Our hearts are glad as we think of Christ's return. While much of what we anticipate will probably be very different from what we imagine, one thing is sure: "We shall see him as he is." "What will you say to him, when you wake up in the next world?" asked a Christian physician as he attended a dying girl. "I will say, 'I know you.' " "For now we see in a mirror dimly, but then face to face" (1 Cor. 13:12).

Discussion Questions

1. Of the following phrases and words used to describe Christ's Parousia, which three, in a strict sense, are not biblical?

The second coming	Rapture	The coming (*parousia*)
The great day	Day of judgment	The appearing (*epiphaneia*)
The return of Christ	Day of redemption	The revelation (*apokalupsis*)
The last day	Day of the Lord	The meeting (*apantesis*)

Those which appear in the Bible can be found in the following texts: Jude 6; John 6:39; Matthew 11:22; Ephesians 4:30; 1 Thessalonians 5:2; Matthew 24:30; 1 Timothy 6:14; 1 Peter 1:7; 1 Thessalonians 4:17.

2. How was the Greek word *parousia* used in the nonreligious sphere, especially politics? How does Paul use it in his letters to the Thessalonian church to refer to the coming of Christ at the end of this age? See especially 1 Thessalonians 2:19, 20; 3:13; 4:15; 5:23; 2 Thessalonians 2:1, 2.

3. On what grounds did John Darby make a case for two comings of Christ at the end of this age? In brief, what was his

scheme? According to the author, this view is dubious. Why?

4. The author says that in the New Testament view of Christ's Parousia, "end-time events are not in focus, but rather the Person of Jesus Christ." Why do you suppose he feels it is necessary to make this point? Can you think of examples in which the attention of Christians has been diverted from the real significance of Christ's coming by speculation about the future?

5. Is there a danger that Christians today are becoming too secular—too satisfied with life in this world—that they lose sight of the end of this age and the coming of Christ? What is the proper attitude for Christians living in this world in light of Christ's future Parousia?

CHAPTER SEVEN

"This Mortal Nature Must Put
on Immortality"

In the year AD 163, Justin, who got the nickname "Martyr," stood together with several of his friends before a Roman judge on account of his faith. The judge, who threatened to have them executed, asked Justin, "Do you suppose that you will rise again and live forever?" With deep confidence Justin replied, "I do not suppose it; I know it."

As a philospher, which he was in his pre-Christian days, Justin might have held to the immortality of the soul, as taught by Plato. But he hardly would have accepted the idea of the resurrection of the body. When Paul came to Athens and preached the resurrection of the dead, the Greek philosophers laughed him to scorn. Some thought he was preaching foreign deities "because he preached Jesus and the resurrection" (Acts 17:18). (They may have thought that *Anastasis* [resurrection] was the female consort of Jesus, the male deity; apparently Jesus and Anastasis were the strange deities.) Ladd says, "The idea of personal immortality would have caused no offense to Greeks, but the idea of bodily resurrection was not a truth they could easily accept."[1]

In the Jewish world the resurrection from the dead was a well-known doctrine, but not every Jew believed it. Perhaps one reason for the confusion was the relative silence of the Old Testament on this subject. To be sure, the Old Testament casts a few rays of light on the resurrection, since the bodily existence was held to be essential to humanity, but they are rather dim. "He will swallow up death for ever, and the Lord God will wipe away tears from all faces" (Is. 25:8). "Thy dead shall live, their bodies shall rise. O dwellers in the dust, awake and sing for joy!" (Is. 26:19).

Daniel knows of a separation of the righteous and the ungodly in the resurrection: "And many of those who sleep in the dust of the earth shall awake, some to everlasting life, and some to shame and everlasting contempt" (12:2). There are several passages which speak of deliverance from Sheol, the abode of the dead (Ps. 16:9-11), but it is not certain that they speak of a resurrection. Several passages that speak of a resurrection have a national restoration of Israel in mind, rather than a resurrection of the dead at the end of the age (e.g., Ezek. 37; Hos. 6:1, 2).

Likewise, "the Qumran texts speak plainly enough of eternal life for the righteous and annihilation for the wicked, but throw no clear light on the question of the resurrection."[2]

While belief in the resurrection had received considerable impetus from the martyrdoms under Antiochus Epiphanes, there was still considerable controversy about it in the days of Jesus. The Samaritans denied a resurrection of the body, as did the Sadducees (Mk. 12:18-27). Paul, in his defense before his countrymen, declared himself a defender of the hope in the resurrection. A storm erupted, and his Pharisaic opponents immediately sided with Paul against the Sadducees (Acts 23:6-9).

But not even among those Jews who believed in the resurrection was there complete agreement. Some insisted that only the righteous would be raised (i.e., the Israelites). Some rabbis even suggested that only those buried in the Holy Land would rise again. That may explain why so many Jews who lived in the Diaspora had burial plots around Jerusalem. It may also explain why Jerusalem had so many widows, since diaspora Jews would tend to move there late in life. Some Jewish views of the resurrection of the body were downright crude and materialistic, and were not derived from the Scriptures.

With the destruction of the Jewish state (AD 70), when all the sects vanished except Pharisaism, belief in the resurrection became an established doctrine of orthodox Judaism. By the time the Mishnah was written up (ca. AD 200), it could be said that among those who have no share in the world to come is "the man who says that the revival of the dead cannot be deduced from Scriptures" (Sanh. xi.1).

We now turn to the New Testament to see what it has to say about the resurrection from the dead. We want to ask, first of all, what the grounds of hope for the resurrection are.

The Certainty of the Resurrection
The Teaching of Jesus and the Apostles

In his confrontation with the Sadducees, who denied the resurrection, our Lord pointed them to that part of the Old Testament which they did accept—the Pentateuch. He argued for the resurrection on the basis of Exodus 3:6. If God was the redeemer of Abraham, Isaac, and Jacob, while these patriarchs lived, then surely he will not have forsaken them now that they are dead. God's covenant faithfulness guarantees them their resurrection.

"Do not marvel at this," said Jesus, "for the hour is coming when all who are in the tombs will hear his voice and come forth, those who have done good, to the resurrection of life, and those who have done evil, to the resurrection of judgment" (Jn. 5:28, 29). Jesus' hearers would not have been surprised to hear Jesus speak about the resurrection of the dead as such. What was new was that the Son of man would call the dead to life on the last day.

According to Jewish opinion, no one could raise the dead except God (cf. 2 Cor. 1:9). What annoyed the Jewish leaders, when the church was established at Pentecost, was not that the apostles preached the resurrection, but that they were proclaiming "in Jesus the resurrection from the dead" (Acts 4:2). The apostles were not preaching merely that the dead would rise, but they were proclaiming a historical event which guaranteed the resurrection of all men.

When Lazarus died and Jesus comforted Martha by assuring her that her brother would rise, she responded: "I know that he will rise again in the resurrection at the last day" (Jn. 11:24). But then Jesus boldly claimed, "I am the resurrection and the life." Jesus was saying in effect that the moment a person puts his trust in Christ he begins to experience the life of the age to come.

Several people who had died were raised by Jesus as signs that the new age had dawned. But they returned to an earthly existence and died again. As far as we know these were resuscitations rather than resurrections. Nevertheless, the raising of Lazarus, the daughter of Jairus, and the son of the widow of Nain was a pledge of the conquest of death by Jesus. The raising of the dead, including those saints who came out of their graves at the resurrection of Jesus, was symbolic of the inbreaking of the kingdom of God, in which there will be no more death (Rev. 20:14; 21:4).

The apostles, in keeping with Jesus' teachings, also proclaimed the resurrection of the just and the unjust (Acts 24:15). The writer to the Hebrews lists the doctrine of the resurrection of the dead among the foundation teachings of the Christian faith (Heb. 6:2). What is new in the teaching of the apostles is that the resurrection of the dead is constantly tied to the resurrection of Jesus.

The Resurrection of Jesus from the Dead

In his earliest correspondence Paul assures the sorrowing Thessalonians that if it is true that God raised Jesus from the dead (and there was no doubt about that), "even so, through Jesus, God will bring with him those who have fallen asleep" (1 Thess. 4:14). When warning the Corinthians not to abuse their liberty by giving their bodies to immorality, Paul reminds them that "God raised the Lord and will also raise us up by his power" (1 Cor. 6:14).

Nowhere, however, is the close connection between the resurrection of the dead and the resurrection of Christ developed so elaborately as in 1 Corinthians 15. "If there is no resurrection of the dead," says Paul, "then Christ has not been raised" (15:13). Since, however, it is an unshakable fact that Christ was raised from the dead, he has become "the first fruits of those who have fallen asleep" (v. 20.)

The word "first fruits" carried a vivid meaning for Jewish Christians. The festival of first fruits marked the beginning of the harvest in the Jewish year. It not only expressed the hope of a harvest, but was the actual beginning of it. So Christ's resurrection, while not followed immediately by the resurrection of the dead, marked the beginning of that great eschatological event.[3]

Just as all humankind died in Adam, so in the new Adam, Christ, all are made alive (v. 22). This deep assurance that "he who raised the Lord Jesus will raise us also with Jesus and bring us with you into his presence" (2 Cor. 4:14), sustained Paul in his greatest trials. Ladd writes, "In the New Testament, the idea and hope of resurrection centers altogether in the resurrection of Jesus. . . . His resurrection means that he has 'abolished death and brought life and immortality to light through the gospel.' "[4]

Karl Heim illustrates in a very picturesque manner the close connection between Christ's resurrection and ours:

> Just as when a dyke in the Low Countries on the shores of the North Sea gives way, even if it is only one little section, we know that, although this is in itself an event of small importance, the consequences are incalculable; beyond the dyke is the tumultuous sea which will burst through the opening—so Paul knew, when he had met the Risen One, that He is the 'first-born of them that slept.'[5]

Jesus is called the "first-born from the dead" (Col. 1:18). This means not only that Jesus was the first to rise from the dead, as Paul told Agrippa (Acts 26:23), but it also means that he now stands at the head of a new humanity and leads others with him into an endless life with God.

The certitude of our hope in the resurrection of the dead rests, first, on the teachings of Jesus and his apostles. More fundamentally it rests on the resurrection of Jesus himself. There is, however, a third foundation stone on which the doctrine of the resurrection from the dead rests, and that is the Holy Spirit.

The Presence of the Holy Spirit

In his Pentecost sermon Peter makes it very clear that the Spirit which was poured out in such abundance was the Spirit of the risen Christ. "This Jesus God raised up. . . . Being therefore exalted at the right hand of God . . . he has poured out this which you see and hear" (Acts 2:32, 33).

Similarly, Paul writes to the Romans: "If the Spirit of him who raised Jesus from the dead dwells in you, he who raised Christ Jesus from the dead will give life to your mortal bodies also through his Spirit which dwells in you" (Rom. 8:11). Farther along in the same chapter Paul calls the Holy Spirit the "first fruits," a kind of foretaste of what is yet to come, namely, "the redemption of our bodies" (8:23).

The hope that what is mortal will some day be swallowed up by life is even now guaranteed to us by the gift of the Spirit (2 Cor. 5:4, 5). This Spirit Paul calls a "down payment," a term which, like first fruits, assures us that there is more to come (cf. Eph. 1:13, 14). By the Spirit we have been sealed for the day of redemption, and that includes the redemption of the body (Eph. 4:30).

By the indwelling of the Spirit, believers can now live in the hope of the resurrection. "It was no mere intimation of immortality that they thus received," says Bruce, "it was an initial experience of immortality, though the full experience must await the parousia."[6]

The First Resurrection

Whereas the New Testament clearly teaches the resurrection of all people, most of the passages which deal with the resurrection speak only of the resurrection of the believer. That is to be expected since the New Testament books were addressed to believers. Paul makes it very plain that the resurrection of the saints takes place at the Parousia of our Lord. "But each in his own order: Christ the first fruits, then at his coming those who belong to Christ. Then comes the end" (1 Cor. 15:23, 24a). Whether the word "end" (*telos*) suggests another resurrection is not clear. It may be only a general reference to the end of the age. Bruce makes the remark: "It is curious—though it may be accidental—that in Paul's letters there is no clear reference to the resurrection of the wicked."[7]

John, however, does divide the resurrection of the dead into two stages (Rev. 20), by putting the millennial reign of the saints between the first resurrection and the resurrection of the dead for the final judgment. "The rest of the dead did not come to life until the thousand years were ended. This is the first resurrection. Blessed and holy is he who shares in the first resurrection! Over such the second death has no power . . ." (Rev. 20:5-6). This first resurrection takes place when Christ returns with the armies of heaven in great glory (Rev. 19:11 ff.).

That this first resurrection, this better resurrection (Heb. 11:35), takes place at the coming of Christ is affirmed in Paul's first letter to the Thessalonians. "For the Lord himself will descend from heaven with a cry of command, with the archangel's call, and with the sound of the trumpet of God. And the dead in Christ will rise first" (4:16).

Similarly, writing to the Philippians, Paul explains that the commonwealth of the believer is in heaven "and from it we await a Savior, the Lord Jesus Christ, who will change our lowly body to be like his glorious body, by the power which enables him even to subject all things to himself" (3:20, 21). It is to this resurrection from the dead at Christ's coming that Paul himself hopes to attain (Phil. 3:11).

But some will ask, as Paul asked, "How are the dead raised? With what kind of body do they come?" (1 Cor. 15:35). We must be satisfied with Paul's answer, although even his answer has been understood differently. If we want to know more about the resurrection body than Paul tells us, our curiosity will go begging. We turn, then, to a discussion of the question of the nature of the resurrection body.

The Resurrection Body

"Flesh and blood cannot inherit the kingdom of God, nor does the perishable inherit the imperishable" (1 Cor. 15:50). The bodies which God gave us for our earthly existence are of flesh and blood, subject to decay and death. Our life in the world to come demands a different kind of body. There is, however, a continuity between this earthly body and the new body which the believer receives when Christ returns. The "I," the "person," which is linked to an earthly body in this life, will survive death and by the resurrection will be linked to a new and glorious body.

Paul illustrates the connection between the earthly and heavenly bodies with a seed which is put in the ground from which springs a plant. On the other hand, he also stresses the radical discontinuity between the kernel that died in the ground and the plant which sprang from it. "What you sow does not come to life unless it dies. And what you sow is not the body which is to be. ... But God gives it a body as he has chosen" (1 Cor. 15:36-38). The illustration from heavenly bodies also stresses that the resurrection body will be different from the one that is left behind. But even though our bodies will be changed from earthly to heavenly bodies, we remain the same personality.

The difference between the earthly body and the resurrection body is described in different ways. The body that goes to the grave is perishable, but the body that is raised is imperishable. "It is sown in dishonor, it is raised in glory. It is sown in weakness, it is raised in power" (1 Cor. 15:42, 43). Indeed, Paul goes so far as to say that the resurrection body will "be like his glorious body," that is, like Christ's (Phil. 3:21).

It should be made very clear that the New Testament does not teach the resurrection of the flesh, but the resurrection of the body. It is reported that the British churchman, Dr. William

Temple, tried desperately to keep up with friends as they climbed a hill, but constantly kept falling behind. Finally he reached the summit and broke out in words of hope, as he thought of the resurrection: "Thank God I do not believe in the resurrection of the *flesh*." (He did, of course, believe in the resurrection of the *body*.)[8]

If this body of flesh were to be perpetuated in the world to come, some of us would be less than optimistic. But because God promises us a new and glorious body, we can be sure that the imperfections and disabilities of our present bodies will not be perpetuated in the beyond. There is a world of difference between a "physical" resurrection (which the Bible does not teach) and a "bodily" resurrection (which it does teach).

Because our bodies have such a high destiny we should be careful not to despise our bodies. That was the error of Gnosticism, and that lead to many aberrations. As a matter of fact, it is because of the hope that our bodies are going to be raised, that Paul argues that the body should be treated with dignity (1 Cor. 6:13, 14). Nevertheless, our earthly bodies are "bodies of humiliation" (Phil. 3:21; not "vile" bodies as the AV has it). They cause us to groan and to wait for "the redemption of our bodies" (Rom. 8:23).

In the resurrection chapter (1 Cor. 15) Paul puts the "physical body" (*soma psychikon*, v. 44) in opposition to the "spiritual body" (*soma pneumatikon*). The former represents man's earthly existence and the latter his post-resurrection life. What some Bible readers find a bit puzzling, as well as disconcerting, is the notion that life in the beyond will be so ethereal (spiritual) that possibly all that is of value to them in their earthly existence will be lost. Lord Boothby put it bluntly: "The thought of a spiritual Mr. Boothby twanging a spiritual harp for eternity has for me limited attraction."

But that is a materialistic way of understanding the term "spiritual body." Paul is not interested in defining for us the substance of which the heavenly body is constituted. His concern is rather with the fact that God determines this new body through the Spirit. To have a spiritual body means to have a personality under the control of the Spirit. Professor Dahl makes the observation that "for St. Paul 'the body' practically means 'the personality.' In this he shows his Hebraic background most clearly ... so that when the Apostle speaks of a 'spiritual body' (*soma pneumatikon*) he means the human personality under the complete control of the Spirit (*pneuma*)."[9]

The new body that will rise will not be subject to the power of sin and death. It will not be subject to the limitations of this earth. It will be a body suited for life in eternity with God, where there will be no more pain, no sickness, no death.

It is sometimes said that our resurrection bodies will be like Christ's body after his resurrection, but prior to his ascension. This must be said with some reservations, for Jesus invited his disciples to touch him and explained: "For a spirit has not flesh and bones as you see that I have" (Lk. 24:39). Moreover, he did have supper with the Emmaus disciples (Lk. 24:30-31). To be sure, he could move through closed doors at will (Jn. 20:19), but his body still had the marks of the nails and the spear. It would be a great disappointment to us if a missing limb in our earthly body should be reflected in our resurrection body.

One explanation of this strange phenomenon is that Jesus was not yet glorified, since he had not yet ascended into heaven. Our bodies shall be transformed at the resurrection to be like his "glorious" body (Phil. 3:21). Another explanation is that he did ascend into glory at the time of his resurrection and that the post-resurrection appearances recorded in the gospels are "condescensions to the earth-bound senses of the disciples."[10]

Not only will the saints who have died receive a new body at the resurrection, but also those who are alive at the coming of the Lord. "We shall not all sleep," says Paul, "but we shall all be changed" (1 Cor. 15:51). (An enterprising scribe, in copying this text, changed the 'not' from the first to the second clause, and so now several important manuscripts read: "We shall all sleep, but we shall not all be changed." However, the reading that we have in the English versions today is the best attested.) This transformation of both the dead and the living saints takes place at the coming of Christ "at the last trumpet. For the trumpet will sound, and the dead will be raised imperishable, and we shall be changed" (1 Cor. 15:52).

Thomas Aquinas tried to harmonize Paul's statement that in Adam all die (1 Cor. 15:22) with 2 Peter 3, where it says that everything on this earth is to be burned. He concluded that all the living would be burned at the coming of Christ and would then be raised from death like all the other dead at the coming of the Lord. That kind of literalism creates more problems than it solves. The transformation of both those who have died and those who are alive at Christ's coming is one that has its beginning here in life, for by the Spirit we are already "changed into his likeness from one degree of glory to another" (2 Cor. 3:18).

There is, however, another side to the doctrine of the resurrection from the dead—a dark and somber aspect. The New Testament teaches not only the resurrection of the just but also that of the unjust. Jesus solemnly announced that the hour would come when all who are in the tombs would hear the voice of the Son of God, "and come forth, those who have done good, to the resurrection of life, and those who have done evil, to the resurrection of judgment" (Jn. 5:29). Those who participate in the first resurrection (Rev. 20:6) are pronounced "blessed," for over them the second death has no more power.

Quite different is the fate of those who reject Christ and who do not participate in the first resurrection at the coming of the Lord. They do not live, according to Revelation 20:5, until the thousand years are ended. Following this transitional period, known as the millennium, the ungodly appear before a great white throne (Rev. 20:11-15). John does not call this a "second resurrection" in contrast to the "first resurrection," but that must be inferred. Nothing is said, however, of the nature of the resurrection bodies of those who are raised to stand before God to be condemned.

John says that those who were not found written in the book of life were thrown into the lake of fire (v. 15), which is the "second death."

In contrast to the bitter end of those who reject the gospel stands the blessed hope of the believer. In his eightieth year, C.H. Dodd, a leading British New Testament scholar, commented in a sermon:

> As our days lengthen the inevitability and finality of death are born in upon us with increasing force. And then we recall that the earthly life of Christ also ended in death. Few life-stories, perhaps, have been written in which the shadow of approaching death is so omnipresent; and the story of its ending has about it all, and more than all, that we should dread in contemplating our own death—all, *except finality*. For his death was not final. There is One at least who has borne our common nature, who succeeded in carrying it unimpaired through death into endless life. [11]

On that first Christian Easter, our Lord rose triumphantly from the grave. Having slain that fierce monster Death, he made a breach in the wall of that great prison house, Death. He now leads the way to an endless life with God, and he asks us to follow.

Discussion Questions

1. Which groups at the time of Christ did not believe in the resurrection of the dead? Note examples in Mark 12:18-27 and Acts 23:6-9. Is the resurrection of the dead an idea unique to the New Testament? What light does the Old Testament cast on this subject? See Isaiah 25:8; 26:19; Daniel 12:2; Psalm 16:9-11.

2. What was it about Jesus' and the apostles' teaching on the resurrection which caused offense to even those who did believe in it? See John 5:28, 29; 11:25, 26; Acts 4:2.

3. The author asserts that there are three foundation stones upon which the hope of future resurrection rests. Can you identify the three? See Acts 4:2; 1 Corinthians 15:20; 2 Corinthians 5:4, 5.

4. How did Paul use the Jewish festival of the first fruits as a

symbol of Christ's resurrection? Consult 1 Corinthians 15:12-20. How did he use the sowing of seed as a symbol of our future resurrection? See 1 Corinthians 15:36-38.

5. Will there be only one resurrection in the future? Or two? Which New Testament writer describes two resurrections?

6. Does the Bible teach a physical or a bodily resurrection? What are some of the word pairs (perishable, imperishable, for example) Paul uses to describe the contrast between our mortal and immortal bodies? See especially 1 Corinthians 15:42-44.

7. One prominent Bible scholar has said, similar to the Lord Boothby quoted by the author, that walking streets of gold and playing a harp for eternity does not appeal to him. He suspects, however, that he'll be able to continue doing those things in heaven which he now enjoys doing on earth which bring glory to God. Do you agree?

CHAPTER EIGHT

"And They Reigned with Christ a Thousand Years"

Judging from the amount of literature on this subject, it would appear to be a central theme of the biblical writers. But this is obviously not the case. Strictly speaking, there is only one reference to the millennium in the entire Bible, and that is Revelation 20:1-10. There are, of course, students of the Scriptures who see in the promises of a glorious future, which the prophets give to the nation of Israel, predictions of a millennium. It is, however, a generally accepted principle of interpretation that the Old Testament must be interpreted in the light of the New, and not vice versa. The New Testament has nothing to say about the restoration of Israel to nationhood. Rather, it sees the fulfillment of Old Testament promises in the new people of God, the church. Therefore, it is not proper, in our view, to carry these so-called "unfulfilled" promises over into Revelation 20. Certainly John makes no allusion to the fulfillment of nationalistic hopes for Israel in the millennial passage. John R. W. Stott wisely said, "I am hesitant about any Old Testament prophecy that is not confirmed in the New Testament."[1]

Some students of Scripture have found an allusion to the millennium in the Parable of the Sheep and the Goats (Mt. 25:31-46). It has been inferred that those nations which treated Israel properly will be allowed to go into the millennium, whereas those who maltreated the Jews will not. This can hardly be the meaning of this parable, for the outcome is clearly stated as either "eternal life" or "eternal punishment."

Whether 1 Corinthians 15:23-26 allows us to insert the millennial period into the text is not certain. Paul speaks of the resurrection of Christ, the firstfruits, followed by the resurrection of the believers at Christ's coming. "Then comes the end." There is an interim between Christ's resurrection and the resurrection of the saints at Christ's return. Whether Paul also has an interim in mind between Christ's return and the "end" *(telos)* is not certain.

Just because there is only one clear reference to the millennium in the New Testament does not mean that we have the freedom to overlook this subject or that it has no significance. It should be remembered, nevertheless, that it is not an article of faith in the early creeds of the church.

Since the millennium has played such an important part in discussion about future things and is still a point of considerable debate and division, it is only right that we should devote a chapter to it.

The Concept of the Millennium

The Greek word for the millennium, the thousand-year reign of Christ, is *chilios* (whence our English 'chiliasm'). The Latin translation of *chilios* is "millennium" (from *mille*—"thousand," and *annus*—"year"). *Chilios* occurs six times in as many verses in Revelation 20.

The Apostle John, who was inspired by God's Spirit to write the Apocalypse, was deeply steeped in Jewish thought. This is reflected in the symbolism, the imagery, and the phraseology of the book. Deeply rooted in Jewish messianic expectations was the hope that God's anointed King would establish an earthly kingdom, elevate Israel to unprecedented greatness, crush the evildoers, and set up a reign of peace and righteousness. This hope stands in vivid contrast to that of some pagan cultures, where the golden age lies in the past. In Israel it always lay in the future. This hope sustained Israel in its darkest hours.

As time went on the traditional hope of the Davidic kingdom was amalgamated with a view that came from apocalyptic circles, in which Messiah comes in clouds of glory and establishes a heavenly kingdom. Out of the fusion of these two concepts emerges the view that before the heavenly kingdom can come there will be an earthly messianic reign of limited duration. This is to be followed by a last assault of evil powers and the beginning of the future world.[2]

The temporary earthly interim was estimated by some to last 400, 600, 1,000, or more years. In 4 Ezra 7:28, 29 the hope is expressed that it will last as long as Israel's affliction in Egypt had lasted (Gen. 15:13—400 years), since the psalmist had prayed, "Make us glad according to the days wherein you have afflicted us and the years wherein you have seen evil."

More popularly it was thought of as a thousand-year transitional reign on earth, prior to the dawn of the eternal kingdom. This earthly reign was often described in fantastically materialistic terms. In 2 Baruch 29:5, 6, for example, it is predicted that "the earth shall yield its fruit ten thousandfold, and on each vine there shall be a thousand branches, and each branch shall produce a thousand clusters, and each cluster shall produce a thousand grapes and each grape a cor [120 gallons/540 liters] of wine."

The notion of a millennial reign, then, was at hand when John wrote the Revelation. John "Christianizes" the term, and so the millennial concept is part and parcel of the divine revelation given to John. It is, therefore, no longer simply a Jewish notion, but a biblical teaching which we should try to understand.

With these brief comments on the concept of the millennium, let us examine the text in Revelation 20 before we discuss the main lines of interpretation.

The Millennial Passage

Revelation 19 closes with an awesome scene. John sees Christ, the Rider on the white horse, followed by the armies of heaven, coming in great glory and majesty for the final battle with the forces of the Beast, the Antichrist. This is quite in line with Paul's description of the coming of Christ in 2 Thessalonians 1:7, 8. In the latter text Christ is portrayed as coming "from heaven with his mighty angels in flaming fire, inflicting vengeance upon those who do not know God and upon those who do not obey the gospel of our Lord Jesus."

All the hosts of evil are vanquished by the sharp sword which comes from Christ's mouth (his word of judgment), so that if we take John seriously there are no living unbelievers left. The arch-enemy of humankind, the Devil, who inspired the Beast and his followers, is then bound and locked up in the abyss for a thousand years. This defeat of all the enemies of God, including Antichrist, and the binding of Satan marks the beginning of the millennial reign.

With the dawn of the millennium, all those who belong to Christ rise from the dead. This is the "first resurrection" (20:5), which takes place at the coming of Christ. So privileged is the lot of those who have died in Christ, and who now come to life, that the seer pronounes a beatitude on all those who have a share in the first resurrection, for "over such the second death has no power" (20:6). It should be remembered, of course, that not all believers will die, but those who are alive at Christ's coming will be transformed together with the resurrected saints (1 Cor. 15:51).

Those who belong to Christ at his coming are then glorified. They sit on thrones—a symbol of rule and authority (v. 4). The question over whom they rule, when all evildoers have been liquidated, does not concern John; it is simply a way of saying that their true kingship will be revealed. This is the fulfillment of Christ's promise to the overcomer: "I will grant him to sit with me on my throne, as I myself conquered and sat down with my Father on his throne" (Rev. 3:21). It is also stated that they are "priests of God and of Christ" (v. 6), a reference to their nature rather than their activity. Several times in the New Testament believers are said to be redeemed by Christ and made "priests" and "kings" (or "kingdom" cf. 1 Peter 2:9; Revelations 1:5; 5:9 f.). The church cannot demonstrate the reality of her kingship or her priestliness during this present time of her pilgrimage. Only when Christ appears will these be brought to light.[3]

Judgment is given to the enthroned saints (20:4). This does not mean that they were judged (although that is stated elsewhere, e.g., 2 Corinthians 5:10), but rather that they do the judging. The background for this language is to be found in Daniel 7:13-22, where the kingdom passes to the saints of the Most High and judgment is given to them. To put it in Pauline terms once again, "Do you not know that the saints will judge the world?" (1 Cor. 6:2). The word "judge," like the word "rule," means nothing more than that they participate with Christ in the final triumph and judgment over all evil powers. Lactantius (4th century) thought some nations would enter the millennium so that the saints who rule with Christ might have someone to rule over.[4] But the word "rule" does not require that.

There are those who wish to restrict the occupants of the thrones which John saw to the twelve apostles (in the light of Mt. 19:28). Others restrict them to the martyred saints (20:4b), but it is best not to be that restrictive. All believers are encouraged again and again by the promise of Jesus that, if they suffer with him here in life, they will reign with him in glory. Among those who reign with Christ are those who were beheaded because they refused to worship the Beast and remained firm in their witness to Christ. All those who remain loyal to Jesus (whether they are actually killed or suffer for his name in other ways) will be exalted with Christ when he comes.

The millennial reign, however, is not yet the ultimate state of glory to which God promises to bring his own. At the end of the thousand years Satan is loosed once more, and his incorrigibly evil character is revealed in that he prepares for a final onslaught on God and his peoples. Since chapter 19 has already described the total destruction of the followers of the Beast, the question has been asked: Who are the evil forces that Satan rallies after the millennium for a final showdown between himself and God?

Some scholars are of the opinion that this last effort by Satan to destroy God's redemptive purposes must be understood as a rebellion of the underworld in which Satan is kept during the millennium. If this is the correct interpretation, then this final revolt of Satan deals with the kingdom of the demonic powers in the underworld. Rissi suggests that Revelation 20:7-10 should be interpreted thus: "Satan entices the ghostly nations of the dead, and the demons, 'innumerable as the sand of the sea,' from the four corners of the earth where the underworld manifests itself, in order to make war on the resurrected ones."[5] God and Magog, then, are not historical nations, but the bands of Hell, similar to the armies of Abaddon which ascend from the bowels of the earth (9:1-11), or the hordes of demons (9:13-19). The unredeemed, with Satan at their head, are then revealed as the enemies of God and the church. No battle takes place, since Christ won the victory long ago. It is simply stated that fire from heaven consumes them.

There are obviously other ways of interpreting this passage, and this has led to quite different understandings of the millennium. Let us look at the main lines briefly.

Interpretations of the Millennium

Postmillennialism

According to this line of interpretation, there is yet to come here on earth a glorious reign of Christ prior to the return of Christ. This reign, in which saints participate, is to come about as more and more people and nations bow to the lordship of Christ.

Since numbers in apocalyptic literature are often symbolic, the thousand years are taken to be the length of that period, prior to Christ's return, when the gospel triumphs in all the world.

The view stems from a very optimistic understanding of history and has given great impetus to evangelism and missions. It holds that the ushering in of this new age here on earth is to a large extent dependent on the church's faithfulness to the Great Commission.

Daniel Whitby (1683-1726) gave this understanding of the millennium its most impressive formulation, although he was not the first to espouse it.[6] The destruction of Antichrist before the millennium was interpreted by him to mean the collapse of the Roman Catholic Church. Pagan religions, Islam, atheism, and secularism would give way to Christ's rule. The Methodist revival in the 18th century contributed considerably to this optimistic view of histroy. Jonathan Edwards, the great American preacher of the 18th century, also espoused this view. Perhaps no one was more instrumental in propagating this view than Matthew Henry of commentary fame.

This understanding of the millennium was probably the most popular in America at the turn of the twentieth century, bolstered by the overwhelming progress Western missionaries were making in "heathen" lands. After the terrible wars and revolutions that the world has witnessed in the 20th century, postmillenialism is not very popular today. It tends to overlook the witness of the New Testament to the increasing darkness as the end draws closer.

Amillennialism

The word is really a misnomer, for it does not mean that the adherents of this interprepation do not believe in a millennium. Rather they understand it to be a spiritual reign of Christ which began with the binding of Satan at Christ's first coming. The thousand years span the entire interim between Christ's first and second coming, since with the Lord a thousand years are like a day. The first resurrection is taken to mean the spiritual resurrection of unbelievers to new life. The kingdom, Christ's reign over his people, is a present reality, and the saints share in this reign. The releasing of Satan after the millennium is equated with the coming of Antichrist prior to Christ's return.

This understanding of the millennium goes back to the early centuries of the Christian church, but was given its classical expression by Augustine (354-430) who brought chiliasm to its demise. Augustine's view reflected the fact that the world had become "Christian" under Constantine. Even though there was much evil left, this was to be expected since Jesus had spoken of tares among the wheat right up to the time of the harvest. So it happened that other millennial views were condemned, and Jerome could write: "Let us have done with this fable of a thousand years."[7] The Augustinian view of the millennium continued to dominate not only the Middle Ages but also the Reformation period, although chiliasm never died out completely. Very popular during the Reformation was the view that the Roman Catholic hierarchy represented Antichrist and that, therefore, the end of the age could not be far away.

Exegetically this understanding of Revelation 20 has fewer problems than the postmillennial interpretation. It is held very widely today by Christians throughout the world.

Premillennialism

According to the premillennial understanding of Revelation 20, the millennium represents an interim or transition between this age and the eternal state. This view is as old as the 2nd century. While it nearly disappeared during the Middle Ages, it was revived during and after the Reformation, although Joachim of Floris (12th century) had already abandoned the Augustinian view. When Justin Martyr in the second century was asked by Trypho the Jew whether he thought the earthly Jerusalem was to be restored, he said yes. But then he added, "on the other hand, I signified to you that many who belong to the pure and pious faith, and are true Christians, think otherwise."[8]

As Justin suggests, there have always been differences of opinion on the nature of the millennium even among those who hold the premillenarian view—a view which is held widely by evangelicals today.[9]

Some of the questions which divide premillennialists are: Will this reign be in heaven or on earth? Will there be people over whom the saints rule? If so, who are they? Are the thousand years to be taken mathematically or do they simply mark off a certain period known only by God as to their length?

Whereas premillennialism is as old as the second century, a special kind of premillennialism was introduced by J. N. Darby (1800-1882). We have mentioned earlier his division of the Parousia into two stages. According to his understanding, an earthly millennium is to be established after Christ's coming in glory with his saints, who will reign with Christ from a reestablished Jerusalem. Some nations will be allowed to enter the millennium. After the conversion of the Jews, who will then serve as effective evangelists, many shall acknowledge Christ as king. At the end of this earthly reign of Christ, in which the Old Testament nationalistic promises to Israel are fulfilled, Satan leads the forces of Evil in a final battle against God. The defeat of these evil powers signals the beginning of the eternal state.

Through his many writings and preaching ministry, Darby's views were spread very widely. D. L. Moody (1837-1899) was converted to his view, and the Bible institute named after him has remained faithful to the founder's understanding of the millennium, as have many other biblical institutes. Perhaps even more influential in spreading Darby's views was C. I. Scofield (1843-1921). Scofield introduced this system of interpretation into the margin of the Scofield Reference Bible, of which millions of copies have been sold in the United States.

It should be remembered, however, that this understanding of the millennium was not held in the first 1,800 years of the church's history. It is to be distinguished from the earlier premillennialism that goes back to the early centuries. This early view of the millennium, which seems to fit best into Revelation 20, is not to be confused with the interpretation of Darby.

In this brief overview of differing lines of interpretation, many questions have been left untouched. No view is free from problems. It would be great gain if we could be, as F. F. Bruce put it, "content to follow the relevant passages of Scripture as they come . . . [and] dispense with interpretative labels; I for my part would not care to wear any of them."[10] This will probably not happen until the millennium arrives. It is unfortunate that different understandings of this concept have led to divisions among Christians who are concerned about being true to the Scriptures.

A question that may well arise in our minds at this point is, whether there is any practical significance in this doctrine of the millennium? Is there something in this teaching that could be preached, or is this merely of academic interest?

The Significance of the Millennium

Professor Ladd confesses that "the New Testament nowhere expounds the theology of the millennium, that is, its purpose in God's redemptive plan."[11] Limiting ourselves to Revelation 20, perhaps at least three inferences can be made.

Evil Conquered

There is no New Testament book that opens up to us such depths of wickedness as the Revelation. The Old Serpent, Satan, represented by the Dragon, rages in all his fury against God and his people. He inspires the Beast who makes totalitarian claims on the lives of men and women. The False Prophet seeks by subtle and sinister methods to deceive the faithful. The church has to wrestle with spiritual superpowers, and suffers at the hands of the Beast's followers.

With the dawn of the millennial reign, however, the Beast and the False Prophet are finally liquidated, and Satan is cast into the abyss and bound. At last this Satanic trinity is put out of commission. And that's good news.

To be sure, the believer experiences deliverance from the power of evil even as he waits for the final overthrow of evil. But what an encouragement it is in our conflicts with sin to know that in the end God will triumph and we will share in this victory!

Wrongs Righted

John sees the souls of those who were beheaded for the

testimony of Jesus and for the Word of God. They lived and
reigned with Christ a thousand years. Here on earth their in-
nocent blood was spilled and God seemed to be silent. They were
condemned unjustly before human courts, and God did not
reverse these wrong judgments. The martyrs under that altar cry:
(Rev. 6) "O Sovereign Lord . . . how long?" Now they get their
final answer. With the binding of Satan and the resurrection of
the dead at the return of Christ, the hour of their vindication has
come. They sit with Christ on his throne.

How much of the wrong perpetrated daily in our world goes
unnoticed! Think of the millions who died innocently in the wars
of this century alone! Think of the economic and racial injustices
which plague our age. One hesitates to mention all the wrongs
done in the name of religion—of the church. The doctrine of the
millennium assures us that someday all wrongs will be righted.

Loyalty Rewarded

The Book of Revelation makes a clear distinction between
the so-called "earthdwellers" who take on the mark of the Beast
and the saints who follow the Lamb wherever he leads. The Beast
(Nero, Domitian, and the whole line of totalitarian rulers which
ends with Antichrist) seeks to crush the followers of the Lamb,
and many of them die because of their loyalty to Jesus.

With the dawn of the millennial kingdom, all those "who
had not worshiped the beast or its image and had not received its
mark on their foreheads and their hands" come to life. Then they
reigned with Christ a thousand years. Their loyalty to Jesus paid
off. Through the cross they attained to the crown.

For saints under the heel of the oppressor, the millennium is
not an academic topic, as it is so often among believers who live in
peace and security, and who have yet to learn what it means to
make costly decisions between Christ and Caesar. For our
brothers and sisters all over the world, languishing in prisons and
slave-labor camps for their witness to Jesus, the millennial
message is good news. To know that in the end God will make all

wrongs right, reward his faithful servants, and triumph over all evil, that is gospel—good news.

Discussion Questions

1. What does the word "millennium" mean? What is the origin of the concept in Jewish thought?

2. How are we to understand the warring of Christ at the end of this age against the ungodly (Rev. 19:11-16; 2 Thess. 1:7, 8) in light of Jesus' teachings on peace during his lifetime (Mt. 5:38 ff.)?

3. Can you name and elaborate on the three major lines of millennial interpretation? Which view emphasizes the efforts of the church at bringing in the millennium? Which view received its classic expression in Augustine? Which view interprets the millennium as a transitional stage between this age and the eternal state? Why do you suppose that the different interpretations of the millennium have been divisive in the Christian church?

4. Does the idea of the millennium have any practical significance for Christians? If so, what? The author says there are three implications of the millennium which deserve the attention of Christians. What are they? Why might oppressed Christians receive more readily the millennial message than Christians who live in relative peace and prosperity? Read Revelations 20:1-10 with oppressed Christians in mind.

5. One millennial interpretation has tended to be so optimistic about human efforts for bringing in the kingdom that it has underestimated the power and pervasiveness of human evil. Another millennial viewpoint tends to be so pessimistic about humanity and history that it devalues efforts at working toward social justice and the common good of all people. How can Christians strike a balance between these two tendencies, recognizing the power of evil while at the same time fulfilling Jesus' command to work at the needs of oppressed and disadvantaged people (Mt. 25:31-46)?

CHAPTER NINE

"And After That the Judgment"

Judgment is not exactly the most palatable subject to write about. We are told that in his later years the evanglist D. L. Moody always wept when he spoke on this theme. Hesitation to pursue this topic arises not only from the awful solemnity of it, but also from the hidden mysteries of this teaching which God has not seen fit to disclose to man. Nevertheless, if we are to be faithful to the Scriptures, we cannot avoid what the writer to the Hebrews calls an "elementary doctrine" (Heb. 6:1, 2).

The Old Testament may contain some dim adumbrations of the doctrine of punishment in the after life, but does not clearly spell it out. The matter changes when we come to the intertestamental period. Sheol, which in the Old Testament is the abode of all the dead, is now divided into Paradise and Gehenna, with evildoers suffering torment in Gehenna.

Some Jewish writers describe the torments of the ungodly after death rather realistically. Men are seen hanging by their hair for letting their hair grow for adornment; by their eyelids for allowing their eyes lustful looks; and those who ate on fast days are forced to eat bitter gall.[1]

This is not too different from descriptions of eternal punishment found in some early Christian writings. In the Apocalypse of Peter those who blasphemed the way of righteousness are seen hanging by their tongues, while the flaming fire torments them from beneath. Women hang by their hair over the bubbling mire, because they adorned themselves for adultery—not to mention even more gruesome pictures.[2]

The New Testament writers are rather more reserved and discreet in their descriptions of eternal punishment. Nevertheless, the doctrine of final judgment is firmly anchored in the New Testament. It is exegetically untenable to accept the biblical teaching on the love and the grace of God and to reject those passages which speak of divine wrath and eternal punishment.

In this chapter we want to examine the writings of the New Testament to discover what they have to say about judgment. Our interest is primarily in eschatological judgment at the end of history. It should not be overlooked, however, that God's wrath is even now "revealed from heaven against all ungodliness and wickedness of men" (Rom. 1:18). In the words of Alan Richardson, "Since the opening scenes of the last drama of world history are now being staged, their preliminary manifestations are already apparent to the eyes of faith."[3]

God's judgments in history are most vividly portrayed in the last book of the Bible. Wars, revolutions, earthquakes, floods, plagues, famines, economic disasters, political chaos and moral degradation are seen as forerunners of the great day of wrath at the end of the age. These judgments of God are mysterious and unsearchable (Rom. 11:32). God restrains his wrath in order to give man an opportunity to turn to God. Once the day of grace is over, however, man must face the Judge of all the earth. This final day of judgment will prove to be a day full of salvation for the believer, but it will be a day of uttermost wrath for the wicked.[4]

Let us look, first of all, at the certainty of judgment to come.

The Certainty of Judgment to Come
The Proclamation of the Forerunner

The great prophets of the Old Testament had proclaimed the coming of the day of the Lord in which the ungodly would be judged. Since Israel thought of herself as God's people, it was popularly thought that the judgment of this day of wrath would strike only the Gentiles. But Amos warned that God would not judge between Israel and the nations, but between the godly and the ungodly, and there were plenty of those in Israel and Judah. Quite contrary to what Israel so blithely expected, namely that the day of the Lord would be a day of light for Israel, Amos stressed that it would be a dark day for sinners in Israel as well as for those of the nations (Amos 5:18 ff.).

John the Baptist's message of judgment was in the tradition of this prophetic understanding, except that John stressed that this final judgment was about to take place; it was imminent. "Even now the axe is laid to the root of the trees" (Mt. 3:10). God is ready to cut down the bad trees and throw them into the fire. He warned his fellow Jews that they would not escape the wrath to come in their present condition. Only by repentance could they hope to be saved from the fire of judgment (Mt. 3:7, 8). Being descendants of Abraham, he declared, would do them no good on the day of reckoning (v. 9).

Also, he proclaimed that the greater One who was to come after him, would baptize not only with the Holy Spirit, but with fire (v. 11). Whereas "fire" may signify a cleansing process, in keeping with Malachi 3:2, 3, in the context of Matthew 3 it is a metaphor for judgment. The coming One would "clear his threshing floor and gather his wheat into the granary, but the chaff he will burn with unquenchable fire" (v. 12).

What John did not realize was that between the baptism with the Spirit (at Pentecost) and the fire of judgment at the end of the age, there was to be a long interim in which God's grace was to be offered to humanity in the preaching of the gospel.[5]

The Teachings of Jesus

When Jesus announced "the acceptable year of the Lord" (Lk. 4:19; cf. Is. 61:1, 2) in the synagogue of Nazareth, he omitted the phrase which follows this promise in Isaiah 61:2, "and the day of vengeance of our God." Was Jesus contradicting what the Baptist had proclaimed? Hardly! Jesus had more to say about the coming judgment than John did, but John's message needed to be put into perspective. Only after the good news had been preached to both Jews and Gentiles, after the day of God's salvation, would judgment come. Some of the severest words about judgment come from Jesus, the kindest man who ever lived on earth.

Much of what Jesus had to say about judgment is found in his parables. In 12 of the 36 longer parables, Jesus depicts the end of the wicked in frightening terms. One of Luke's parables which immediately comes to mind is the Parable of the Rich Man and Lazarus (Lk. 16:19-31). The rich man thought he was a true son of Abraham (since he was a Jew), but he had paid no attention to the law and the prophets in which concern for the needy is stressed. He thought at first that a mistake had been made and so appealed to "father Abraham." But the answer he got makes it plain that he was no true son of Abraham, since he had disregarded God's Word, and he must now suffer torment.

In Matthew's Gospel the parable of the sheep and the goats (Mt. 25:31-46) stands out as a parable that teaches judgment unequivocally. The ungodly, whose deeds betrayed that they were not true disciples, are banished from the presence of the divine Judge and go away into eternal fire, "prepared for the devil and his angels" (25:41).

Not in parable only, however, did Jesus speak of judgment to come. Jesus warned against sins that can lead people to hell (Mt. 5:22, 29, 30). Every tree, he says, that fails to bring forth good fruit, is cut down and cast into the fire (Mt. 7:19). In commending the faith of the centurion, Jesus said, "The sons of the kingdom will be thrown into the outer darkness; there men will weep and gnash their teeth" (Mt. 8:12). The well-known passage from the fourth Gospel, John 3:16, makes it very plain that those who do not believe shall perish, as opposed to those who receive eternal life. Jesus foresees the day when the dead will hear the voice of the Son of God "and come forth, those who have done good, to the resurrection of life, and those who have done evil, to the resurrection of judgment" (Jn. 5:29).

Alan Richardson writes: "There can be no doubt at all that Jesus taught the dread reality of the last judgment ... only a certain kind of degenerate Protestant theology has attempted to contrast the wrath of God with the mercy of Jesus."[6]

Jesus not only taught that judgment would strike the sinful in the end, but he died in order to save sinners from the wrath of God. And all the apostles agree with Jesus in their emphasis on the coming judgment on the wicked.

The Message of the Apostles

In his memorable sermon before the Areopagus, Paul stressed, among other things, that the God who created all things has appointed a day in which "he will judge the world in righteousness" (Acts 17:31). In his defense before Felix, Paul spoke of justice and self-control and "future judgment" (Acts 24:25), so that the governor became alarmed.

Not only in missionary sermons, but both in his earlier as well as his later letters to the churches, the judgment theme seems to be on Paul's mind. In his first letter to the Thessalonians, he assures his converts that Christ delivers them from the wrath to come (1:10). Even more explicit is the doctrine of judgment in Paul's second letter to the Thessalonians. He speaks of the divine vengeance that God will inflict on the ungodly and then adds: "They shall suffer the punishment of eternal destruction and exclusion from the presence of the Lord and from the glory of his might" (2 Thess. 1:9).

Writing to the Corinthians Paul cautions them against judging before the Lord comes, who will bring to light the secrets of men's hearts (1 Cor. 4:5). And in view of the fact that saints shall participate with Christ in the judgment of the world and of angels (6:2, 3) he urges the Corinthians not to take believers to court.

Perhaps nowhere is Paul's teaching on judgment developed so fully as in his letter to the Romans. Impenitent man, he declares, stores up wrath for himself "on the day of wrath when God's righteous judgment will be revealed" (2:5). For the factious and disobedient there will be "wrath and fury" (v. 8). "There will be tribulation and distress for every human being who does evil, the Jew first and also the Greek" (v. 9). The death and resurrection of Jesus are the guarantee that the believer will be saved from "the wrath of God" (5:9).

The Prison Epistles also strike the note of judgment. The enemies of the cross have no other prospect but "destruction" (Phil. 3:19). To the Ephesians Paul writes that "we were by nature children of wrath" (2:3). "The wrath of God comes upon the sons of disobedience" (Eph. 5:6). Even the Pastoral Epistles speak of judgment (1 Tim. 5:24; 2 Tim. 4:1, 2).

Peter, John, James, Jude, and the unknown author of the Epistle to the Hebrews all share with Paul the understanding that God will judge the wicked (2 Pet. 3:7; Jas. 5:9; 1 Jn. 4:17; Jude 7; Heb. 10:31). Nowhere, however, is judgment portrayed in such vivid colors as in the last book of the Bible, where the last judgment is called "the great day of their wrath" (6:17). All evildoers are condemned finally to the lake of fire (20:15). From the Baptist's cry in the wilderness, up to the shattering music of the Apocalypse, we hear judgment proclaimed loud and clear.

Professor Wenham writes: "Jesus and his disciples taught again and again in terrible terms that there is an irreversible judgment and punishment of the unrepentant. Warnings and loving invitations intermingle to encourage us to flee the wrath to come."[7]

Fully persuaded of the certainty of judgment to come, let us see what the New Testament writers have to say about this great day of reckoning.

The Coming Day of Judgment
The Time

Though we do not have a chronological map of the end of the age laid out before us in the New Testament, the great day of judgment is consistently related to the return of Christ and the circumstances which accompany his Parousia. To be sure, Hebrews 9:27 has it that it is appointed unto man once to die and after that the judgment, but that need not mean that the final judgment takes place at death. By contrast, Peter says that the ungodly are kept "under punishment until the day of judgment" (2 Pet. 2:9).

Our Lord introduced the parable on final judgment (Mt. 25:31-46) with the words, "When the Son of man comes in his glory, and all the angels with him, then he will sit on his glorious throne. Before him will be gathered all the nations" (v. 31).

Paul also connected the final judgment with the coming of Christ in glory. The day of the Lord, he said, would come as a thief in the night for those who belong to the darkness and who then will suffer "sudden destruction" (1 Thess. 5:3). He uses somewhat different imagery in 2 Thessalonians 1:7, 8, but again he connects judgment with the return of Christ, "When the Lord Jesus is revealed from heaven with his mighty angels in flaming fire, inflicting vengeance upon those who do not know God and upon those who do not obey the gospel of our Lord Jesus." In his second letter to Timothy the apostle charges his co-worker "in the presence of God and of Christ Jesus who is to judge the living and the dead, and by his appearing and his kingdom" (4:1).

In the last book of the Bible, the millennial reign, which is inaugurated by the return of Christ (Rev. 19:11-21), precedes the final judgment (20:11-15). However, that does not alter the consistent teaching of the New Testament writers that the judgment of all humanity takes place at the return of Christ.

We know little about the intermediate state of the righteous, between death and resurrection, and even less about the intermediate state of the wicked. But we do know that when Christ appears he will judge the living and the dead (2 Tim. 4:1, 2).

The Judge

The final judgment of humanity is ascribed either to God or to Jesus Christ. Believers are to appear before "the judgment seat of Christ" (2 Cor. 5:10) or "the judgment seat of God" (Rom. 14:10). Obdurate sinners are exposed both to the "wrath of the Lamb" (Rev. 6:16) and "the wrath of God" (Jn. 3:36). The Son of man will sit on his glorious throne and judge the nations (Mt. 25:31). On the other hand, God sits on the great white throne in the final judgment of humanity (Rev. 20:11).

That there is no distinction between the judgment of God and Christ can be seen also from passages where God is said to judge the world by his Son, Jesus Christ. To the Athenians Paul declared that God "has fixed a day on which he will judge the world in righteousness by a man whom he has appointed" (Acts 17:31)—no doubt the Son of man of Daniel 7:13 f. And he goes on to explain that this man is the One he raised from the dead. Similarly, in Romans 2:16 Paul speaks of the day when "God judges the secrets of men by Christ Jesus."

Perhaps the strongest affirmation of the unity of Father and Son in the final judgment is Jesus' saying that "the Father judges no one, but has given all judgment to the Son" (Jn. 5:22). This was new for Jesus' audience, for there is no passage in Jewish literature that unambiguously states that Messiah will be the judge of all mankind; God alone is Judge (Gen. 18:25).[8] Jesus meant that God has delegated his prerogative of judging humanity to his Son. Jesus had said earlier that the Father had given all things into his Son's hand (Jn. 3:35) and that included judgment.

It is because he is the Son of man that God has given him the authority to be the judge (Jn. 5:27). "Son of man" in the context probably means more than this Semitic idiom does at times mean, namely, "man." Being man does not by itself qualify anyone to be the final judge. Rather, it is because Jesus is the Son of man of Daniel 7:13, 14, to whom God gives an everlasting dominion, that he has been given the prerogative to be the judge of all the earth. "The unity of the Father and the Son in judgment as in salvation is as axiomatic for Paul as it is for the Fourth Evangelist," says Bruce.[9]

On the great day of God, Christ, together with his saints and holy angels (Mt. 16:27; 1 Cor. 6:2), will judge the living and the dead. Among those who will not be able to stand in the judgment of God are several categories of evildoers.

The Condemned
The Devil and His Henchmen

The archenemy of humankind, Satan, who deceived our first parents and who led humanity into sin and death, will receive his just reward. In a vision the Seer of Patmos sees a mighty angel who "seized the dragon, that ancient serpent, who is the Devil and Satan, (Rev. 20:2) and bound him for a thousand years and threw him into the pit, and shut it and sealed it over him." (Rev. 2, 3). In the end, however, he is cast into the lake of fire and brimstone (Rev. 20:10). Indeed, the eternal fire, as Jesus explained, was "prepared for the devil and his angels" (Mt. 25:41).

Satan's chief agent in opposing God's work is Antichrist, "the man of lawlessness" (2 Thess. 2:3), "the Beast" (Rev. 13). He too will be liquidated when Christ comes. "And the Lord Jesus will slay him with the breath of his mouth and destroy him by his appearing and his coming" (2 Thess. 2:8). John the apostle sees the Beast in the lake of fire and brimstone together with the Devil. Here they are "tormented day and night for ever and ever" (Rev. 20:10). Evil angels are even now reserved "in the nether gloom until the judgment of the great day" (Jude 6; 2 Pet. 2:4).

What is of greater concern to us, however, is the judgment of humankind.

Wicked Humankind

When Christ returns there will be a great separation of humankind. Those who belong to Christ will enter into his eternal kingdom, the rest will be condemned. This separation is protrayed in various ways. John the Baptist described God's judgment in terms of a Palestinian harvest scene. The wheat is gathered into the granary and the chaff is burned with fire (Mt. 3:12). Jesus used similar imagery in the Parable of the Wheat and the Tares (Mt. 13:4-43) and that of the Dragnet (Mt. 13:47-50). We have already mentioned the Parable of the Sheep and the Goats (Mt. 25) in which a great separation takes place when the Son of man comes in his glory—some going into the eternal kingdom, others into eternal fire.

Those who are condemned on the day of judgment are identified in different ways. First, there are the evildoers. Jesus said that in the end "the Son of man will send his angels, and they will gather out of his kingdom all . . . evildoers, and throw them into the furnace of fire; there men will weep and gnash their teeth" (Mt. 13:41, 42). Similarly, Paul says that "there will be tribulation and distress for every human being who does evil, the Jew first and also the Greek" (Rom. 2:9). Only those who put their trust in Christ will be delivered from the wrath to come (1 Thess. 1:10).

Peter warns his readers against licentious living since they must all give account to him who is ready to judge the living and the dead (1 Pet. 4:3-5). Similarly John, in the Apocalypse, distinguishes Christ's followers who have been redeemed from the earth (14:3) from the "earthdwellers" who take on the mark of the Beast (13:12-18). These wicked "earthdwellers" rejoice at the death of God's faithful witnesses (11:10). But when the great day of God's wrath comes they shall call on the mountains and rocks to fall on them and to hide them from him who is seated on the throne and from the wrath of the Lamb (6:16). At the end of the book, the apostle hears the One upon the throne say that the lot of the "cowardly, the faithless, the polluted . . . murderers, fornicators, sorcerers, idolaters and all liars . . . shall be in the lake that burns with fire and sulphur, which is the second death" (21:8).

Second, Jesus and the apostles make it very clear that all those who reject the gospel and the Christ proclaimed in it shall be condemned on the day of judgment. "He who believes in him," Jesus explained, "is not condemned; he who does not believe is condemned already, because he has not believed in the name of the only Son of God" (Jn. 3:18). Salvation and damnation are contingent on how people respond to Christ.

In the same manner Paul warns of judgment on "those who do not know God and upon those who do not obey the gospel of our Lord Jesus" (2 Thess. 1:8). "For those who are factious and do not obey the truth . . . there will be wrath and fury" (Rom. 2:8). Peter declares that judgment is to begin with the household of God; and if that is so, he asks, "What will be the end of those who do not obey the gospel of God?" (1 Pet. 4:17). He shudders to contemplate the fate of those who have heard the good news of God's saving grace and have rejected it.

A question that naturally arises at this point is, how God will judge those who have never heard the gospel. It is a question the New Testament writers never address. There is, of course, no salvation outside of Christ, "for there is no other name under heaven given among men by which we must be saved" (Acts 4:12).

That there will be degrees of punishment, depending on obedience to the light a person has, seems to be clearly suggested. "All who have sinned without the law will also perish without the law, and all who have sinned under the law will be judged by the law" (Rom. 2:12). Jesus said: "That servant who knew his master's will, but did not make ready or act according to his will, shall receive a severe beating. But he who did not know, and did what deserved a beating, shall receive a light beating" (Lk. 12:47, 48).

Some Bible readers have felt that, on the basis of 1 Peter 3:19 and 4:6, those who have not heard the gospel will be given a chance to decide at death (not a "second" chance, but a "first"). This view is hard to sustain exegetically. Recently Clark Pinnock wrote in *Eternity* magazine, "Of one thing we can be certain: God will not abandon in hell those who have not known and therefore have not declined His offer of grace. Though He has not told us the nature of His arrangements we cannot doubt the existence and goodness of them."[10]

I am not sure that it is wise to go out on a limb in such weighty matters. We must, I think, simply confess with Abraham, "Shall not the Judge of all the earth do right?" (Gen. 18:25). I. Howard Marshall's comments on this subject seem to us to be worth pondering. After conceding that the New Testament does not speculate on this question, he says:

> Nevertheless, there are hints that the heathen will be judged according to how they have responded to the light which they have had. There are some grounds for holding that men whose way of life was such that they would have accepted Christ if they had had the opportunity to do so will be saved at the last day, because the sacrifice of Christ avails for them also (Mt. 25:31 ff.; Rom. 2:12-16). We can safely entrust them to the great mercy and utter justice of God who desires that all men should be saved and come to a knowledge of the truth (1 Tim. 2:4).[11]

The Apostates

A third category among those condemned in the final judgment are the apostates. The warning against apostasy is sounded here and there throughout the New Testament, but no one has underscored the possibility of falling away from the living God as much as the unknown author of the epistle to the Hebrews (Heb. 3:12).

He warns that those who are once enlightened, who have become partakers of the Holy Spirit, and who then commit apostasy, cannot be restored to repentance. They are like the land that bears thorns and thistles, "its end is to be burned" (6:8). Again in chapter 10:26, 27, he declares, "For if we sin deliberately after receiving the knowledge of the truth, there no longer remains a sacrifice for sins, but a fearful prospect of judgment, and a fury of fire which will consume the adversaries." To have received the knowledge of the truth and then to reject it, is to abandon the only way of salvation and consequently to "fall into the hands of the living God" (10:31).

Peter also speaks of those who once escaped the defilements

of the world "through the knowledge of our Lord and Savior Jesus Christ" (2 Pet. 2:20), but who are now entangled in them again. "It would have been better for them never to have known the way of righteousness than after knowing it to turn back from the holy commandment delivered to them" (v. 21). Apparently the writer has false teachers in mind who had once been orthodox Christians, but "like the men of Hebrews 10:26 they have apostatized."[12] While Peter does not describe the end of these apostates, he does say it will be worse than for those who never knew "the way of righteousness."

Since many of these warnings about judgment to come are found in letters to churches, it seems rather obvious that the apostles want the readers to make their calling and election sure (2 Pet. 1:10). Jesus warned at the close of the Sermon on the Mount that many would say to him on that day, " 'Lord, Lord, did we not prophesy in your name, and do many mighty works in your name?' And then will I declare to them, 'I never knew you; depart from me, you evildoers' " (Mt. 7:22, 23). The doctrine of eternal punishment is not merely given for the sake of information about the end of the wicked. It is designed rather to call the professing Christian to examine himself whether he has a living faith that leads to a godly life and noble deeds.

Discussion Questions

1. The author says that God's wrath is already being manifest in the world against evil. Where in the world in the recent past do you see evidence of this?

2. What was the distinctive point in Amos' and John the Baptist's teaching on judgment? What warning did they give to the unfaithful in Israel? See Amos 5:8 ff. and Matthew 3:7-10.

3. Why must the ungodly face judgment? See the following passages: Matthew 25:31-46; John 5:28, 29; Romans 2:1-9; Revelation 20:12. Who is it that will receive condemnation at the final judgment? Check out Matthew 13:41, 42; 25:41; John 3:17, 18; Romans 2:8, 9; 2 Thessalonians 2:8; Hebrews 3:12; 10: 26, 27;

1 Peter 4:3-5; Jude 6; Revelation 20:10. Will Christians have to face judgment? See Romans 14:10; 2 Corinthians 5:10; 1 Peter 4:17.

4. The author raises the question about how persons will be judged who never heard the gospel. Some of the relevant texts are Genesis 18:25; Matthew 25:31 ff; Luke 12:47, 48; Acts 4:12; Romans 2:12-16; 1 Timothy 2:4; 1 Peter 3:18, 19; 4:6. It would be helpful to consult several commentaries on these verses before drawing final conclusions on this subject. Do you agree with the comment by I. Howard Marshall quoted in this chapter? Does the view that the "heathen" will have an opportunity to hear the gospel before the judgment discourage missionary endeavors?

CHAPTER TEN

"And They Will Go Away into Eternal Punishment"

Adolphe Monod confessed that he had tried hard to avoid seeing eternal suffering in the Bible, but that he had not been successful in his efforts. "I gave in; I bowed my head; I put my hand over my mouth; I made myself believe in eternal suffering."[1]

While there is much about heaven and hell that we do not know, we must, as John R. W. Stott writes, be clear and definite "that hell is an awful, eternal reality. It is not dogmatism that is unbecoming in speaking about the fact of hell; it is glibness and frivolity. How can we think about hell without tears?"[2]

In our previous chapter we dealt in general with the subject of judgment at the end of history. In this chapter we want to focus more specifically on several aspects of the biblical teachings regarding eternal punishment. We do this, not because the subject is so delectable, but out of faithfulness to the teachings of our Lord and his apostles.

Since the structure of this universe shall be dissolved when this age comes to an end, it would be gratuitous to try to locate the place where the wicked shall be punished. Nevertheless, the New Testament does speak of a place of torment, as it does of a place of bliss. Let us look, first, at several names and images which describe this place which we call "hell."

The Place of Torment

Gehenna

The word which is most commonly translated into English as "hell" is a Hebrew word, *ge-hinnom*, which is found in its Greek form in the New Testament as *geenna*. *Ge-hinnom* meant originally the "Valley of Hinnom" located southeast of the city of Jerusalem. This valley was a place of ill-repute since the days of Ahaz and Manasseh, when children were sacrificed here to Molech. King Josiah destroyed the pagan shrine in this valley and forbade the worship of Molech, but it remained a desecrated place, despised by all Jews. Indeed, so detestable was the place, that the Valley of Hinnom became Jerusalem's garbage dump. The fire and smoke that emerged from the offal and the trash burned there, and the words of judgment that hung over this valley, made it a fit symbol of the last judgment. In the apocryphal book of First Enoch we read: "This accursed valley is for those who are accursed forever" (27:2). By New Testament times Gehenna has become the word for the eschatological place of torment.

Of the twelve occurrences of the word Gehenna in the New Testament, eleven are found in the mouth of Jesus. Three times in short succession in the Sermon on the Mount our Lord warns those whose lives are characterized by hate and lust, that they are in danger of going to hell (Mt. 5:22, 29, 30). The warning against the evil eye (Mt. 5:29) is repeated in a different context in Matthew 18:9. In Mark's Gospel also we have Jesus' warning against sin underscored by a thrice repeated reference to hell (Mk. 8:43, 45, 47). (Other references to hell are found in Matthew 10:28; Luke 12:5; Matthew 23:25, 33.)

Another word which has been translated as "hell" in some English versions is the Greek word *Hades* (Hebrew: *Sheol*). There may be a few passages in which Hades is used somewhat as an equivalent to Gehenna (cf. Lk. 16:23; Mt. 11:23; Lk. 10:15), but the word is normally reserved for the abode of the dead. Jeremias holds that Hades is not used in the New Testament as a place of punishment in the last judgment.[3] Etymologically, the word Hades means simply the "unseen world" and is used to designate the grave and the world of the dead generally.

Of the fallen angels it is said that God did not spare them but "cast them into hell" (2 Pet. 2:4). All this is expressed in a single verb (*tartaroō* in Greek)—a word which occurs only here in the Bible and means to consign to Tartarus. This word comes from Greek mythology and designates the place where the departed spirits of the most wicked are punished. It has more or less the same meaning for the Greeks that Gehenna had for the Jews. Tartarus was thought of as the lowest and most terrible hell, in which those who rebelled against Zeus were kept. Peter uses it to describe the place where the evil angels are kept as they await final judgment.

In the same sentence (2 Pet. 2:4) the apostle uses another term: "Pits of nether gloom" or "chains of darkness" (depending on whether one reads *sirois*—"pits," silos or *serois*—"chains of darkness—the manuscript evidence is divided). "Pits of darkness" makes better sense and well suits the idea of Tartarus as the lowest depths of Hades. Jude, however, does speak of "fetters of darkness" (v. 6), and that may be what Peter had in mind. It is not, however, the same word which is at times translated as "bottomless pit." That is the translation of some English versions of the Greek word *abyssos* (abyss). The abyss is that dark underworld where the demons are kept prior to their ultimate consignment to the lake of fire (Lk. 8:31), from where the Beast arises (Rev. 11:7), and where Satan is bound and locked up for a thousand years (Rev. 20:1).

One other descriptive term is used to designate the place of eternal torment, "the lake of fire," found a half-dozen times in the Book of Revelation. In extra-Biblical Jewish writings the idea of punishment by fire is common. 1 Enoch 54:1 speaks of the place of judgment as "a deep valley with burning fire." The Apostle John nowhere uses the word Gehenna but, instead, calls the place where the wicked are punished "the lake of fire" (Rev. 19:20;

20:14; 20:15) or "fire and sulphur" (Rev. 20:10; 21:8). This lake of fire does not signify a fate of ultimate annihilation but "torturous existence in the society of evil in opposition to life in the society of God."[4]

There has been much debate on whether "fire," when used of final punishment, is figurative or literal. That debate contributes little to our understanding of this awesome subject. Quite obviously when supra-earthly realities are described—and that holds for heaven as much as for hell—the biblical writers have to use earthly imagery to convey something that lies beyond the grasp of creatures living in this age. What is more frightful here on earth than to be thrown into a furnace of fire? We are, therefore, not surprised to find Gehenna described as a place of burning.

Jesus spoke of "the hell of fire" (Mt. 5:22). In the parable of the wheat and the tares, as well as that of the dragnet, the evildoers are described as being cast into a "furnace of fire" (Mt. 13:42, 50). And those who are set to the left in the parable of the great assize hear the frightening words of the Judge, "Depart from me, you cursed, into the eternal fire prepared for the devil and his angels" (Mt. 25:41).

This Gehenna of fire is also a place of darkness. In intertestamental literature (4 Ezra 7:92; 1 Enoch 63:10; Ps. Sol. 14:9; 15:10; Wis. 17:21) the place of final torment is described as a place of darkness. In rabbinic literature darkness is one of the names given to Gehenna.[5] The writers of the New Testament stand in this literary tradition.

While John uses the terms light and darkness more often than other biblical writers, it is Matthew who uses the term "darkness" most often to describe the place of eternal punishment.[6] He reports Jesus as saying that "the sons of the kingdom will be thrown into the outer darkness" (Mt. 8:12) because of unbelief. In this place of darkness "men will weep and gnash their teeth" (Mt. 8:12; 22:13; 25:30). And that calls for a brief discussion on the nature of the punishment of the wicked.

The Nature of the Punishment

The English Medieval churchman, Bede, described a person in hell with flames of fire gushing out from his ears and eyes and nostrils and at every pore.[7] In Dante's *The Divine Comedy* the fate of the damned is drawn in the most lurid colors. Also, the great eighteenth-century New England preacher, Jonathan Edwards, spoke of an angry God holding the damned over a lake of fire and brimstone as one would hold a loathsome spider over a fire. Examples could be multiplied, but this kind of language resembles more the Jewish apocalypses and later Christian apocryphal writings than the writings of the Scriptures. The biblical writers do not take that kind of liberty in describing the fate of the lost as did, for example, the hymn writer, Isaac Watts. Here is a sample: "What bliss will fill the ransomed souls, When they in glory dwell, To see the sinner as he rolls, In quenchless flames of hell."

We must turn from such human imaginations to the New Testament. Here the fate of the wicked can be viewed from the standpoint of divine wrath, as well as from the perspective of the suffering which the condemned must endure.

The Wrath of God

The Greek New Testament has primarily two words for divine wrath: *thumos* and *orge*. *Thumos* is used of human anger in the writings of Paul (Romans 2:8 is an exception), Luke, and Hebrews; but in the Revelation John uses it repeatedly for divine wrath. There is a reference to vials of wrath (15:7; 16:1), and to the cup of wrath (14:19), and to the wine of God's wrath (14:10; 16:19; 19:15). God is represented as giving the wicked a cup of wrath to drink.[8]

The other Greek word for wrath is *orge*. Staehlin writes that "one could well say that *thumos*, to which there cleaves the idea of outbursting passion, is well suited for the representation of the vision of the seer, but not as designation for the Pauline conception of the wrath of God."[9] *Thumos* more readily denotes passionate anger, whereas *orge* is adapted to a more settled emo-tion.[10] While *thumos* is used only once of divine anger outside the Apocalypse, *orge* is the word used throughout the New Testament to denote God's wrath. It is primarily an eschatological concept.

To tone down the notion of an angry God it has been sug-gested that "wrath" often appears independent of God, making it impersonal. But F. V. Filson insists that "it is unwarranted to separate wrath from God, personalize it, and so make it a personal power independent of God ... Paul was not thinking of a separate being called Wrath."[11] It is not enough to speak of God's wrath as an inevitable process of cause and effect in a moral universe. The wrath of God is the wrath of a divine personality.

There are those who think it is unworthy of God to speak of his wrath. If wrath is understood in terms of the rage of pagan deities, whose anger can be turned to benevolence by suitable of-ferings, then it is indeed unworthy to use the term. If, however, we think of God's wrath as the implacable divine hostility to everything that is evil, then it is impossible to expunge this con-cept from our image of God. God's wrath is not to be understood simply as a "feeling," but as describing the way God reacts toward sin and sinners. It is his personal reaction against sin.[12]

John the Baptist warned his contemporaries that unless they repented they had no hope of escaping from God's coming wrath (Mt. 3:7). Jesus declared that God's wrath rested upon the un-believer already in the present (Jn. 3:37). Paul, too, knows of the present reality of God's wrath (Rom. 1:18; Eph. 2:3), but he also speaks of it as a coming wrath (1 Thess. 1:10; Eph. 5:6). Filson writes: "God's wrath is the necessary reaction of a righteous being against sin. It expresses itself partly in the present, but sometimes is withheld temporarily for purposes connected with God's plan. ... But the most important expression of wrath is that to come at the last day."[13]

On the day of wrath evildoers will be repaid (*apodidomi*) ac-cording to their works (Mt. 16:27; Rom. 2:6; 2 Tim. 4:14; Rev. 18:6; 22:12). This repayment of the wicked for their evil deeds is described as divine vengeance (*ekdikesis*). The Lord is an avenger (*ekdikos*) of all iniquity (1 Thess. 4:6), and so when the last day comes he will inflict "vengeance upon those who do not know God and upon those who do not obey the gospel" (2 Thess. 1:8).

In his wrath God will "punish" the wicked. "They shall suffer the punishment [*dike*] of eternal destruction" (2 Thess. 1:9). Another word for punishment, found only twice in the New Testament, is *kolasis*. It is the modern Greek word for hell. Those who are set on the left in the day of judgment go into "eternal punishment" (Mt. 25:46).

The Suffering of the Ungodly

First, those who are condemned by the divine Judge will be excluded forever from his presence. "I never knew you; depart from me, you evildoers" (Mt. 7:23), will be the awful words of judgment spoken on the last day. The foolish virgins who arrive when the door is shut must hear the frightful words, "Truly, I say to you, I do not know you" (Mt. 25:12). In another parable of Jesus, the householder has locked the door and will not listen to the pleas to open it again. "I tell you, I do not know where you come from; depart from me, all you workers of iniquity!" (Lk. 13:27) are his words. And those who are put to the left in the parable of the sheep and the goats hear the dreadful words, "Depart from me, you cursed" (Mt. 25:41).

Even more explicit is Paul in 2 Thessalonians 1:9: "They shall suffer the punishment of eternal destruction and exclusion from the presence of the Lord and from the glory of his might."

John in his vision of the Holy City, in which the saints dwell with God, expresses the same somber thought by placing all the ungodly "outside" God's dwelling place (Rev. 22:15).

To be banned irrevocably and forever from the presence of God is utter tragedy. In the words of Helmut Thielicke: "To be in hell simply means to be utterly separated from God, but in such a way that one is compelled to see him, that one must see him as a thirsty man sees a silvery spring from which he dare not drink.

This is hell; to be forced to see the glory of God and have no access to it."[14]

Second, those who are condemned experience eternal death. Even "natural" death is viewed by the biblical writers as a judgment of God, and not simply as a law of nature. But physical death does not exhaust God's judgment. "It is appointed for men to die once, and after that comes judgment" (Heb. 9:27).

To make it very clear that there is a death beyond physical death, John in the Revelation speaks of "the second death" (2:11; 20:6, 14; 21:8). It is a rabbinic term, used for the death of the wicked in the next world.[15] In Revelation 20:14 it is identified as the lake of fire; in 21:8 it is the final lot of the ungodly. Those who share in the first resurrection need not fear this second death (20:6). The suffering saints in Smyrna are assured that the second death cannot hurt the overcomer (2:11). This is in harmony with the promise of Jesus, "Truly, truly, I say to you, if any one keeps my word, he will never see death" (Jn. 8:51). Physical death, as the end of our existence here on earth, is tragic enough; what then shall we say about the utter hopelessness of those who are raised only to experience the "second death," which is eternal?

Third, the wicked are said to suffer destruction. One of the verbs used in the New Testament to describe eternal destruction is *apollumi* (occurs 90 times) and the noun *apoleia* (occurs 18 times). While the words are used frequently in the literal or metaphorical sense for human disaster, ruin, downfall, and lostness, they are used also as the opposite of salvation and eternal life. *Apollumi* and *apoleia* mean "definite destruction, not merely in the sense of the extinction of physical existence, but rather of an eternal plunge into Hades and a hopeless destiny of death."[16]

And just as eternal life is both a present possession and a future hope, so "to perish," "to be lost" is both a present tragedy (1 Cor. 1:18) and a future disaster. Destruction awaits those who refuse to repent (2 Pet. 3:9), who reject the truth (2 Thess. 2:10), who are on the broad road that leads to destruction (Mt. 7:13), who are the enemies of the cross (Phil. 3:18).

Another word used to depict the eternal "destruction" of the ungodly is *olethros*. Occasionally the two words (*apoleia* and *olethros*) are found as a word-pair (1 Tim. 6:19). "In 1 Thessalonians 5:3 *olethros* refers to eschatological destruction, suddenly breaking into a situation of apparent security and surprising men like labour pains coming upon a pregnant woman," says Hahn.[17] This destruction is eternal (2 Thess. 1:9).

Fourth, hell is a place of sorrow and pain. Jesus warned those who now laughed, indifferent to the call of the gospel, that in the future they would "mourn and weep" (Lk. 6:25). Jesus speaks of hell also as a place of "gnashing of teeth" (Mt. 8:12; 13:42, 50; 22:13; 24:51; 25:30; Lk. 13:28). This is not an expression of rage, but of extreme suffering and remorse. "It simply denotes the despairing remorse which shakes their whole body. . . ."[18]

In his reference to these terrors, Jesus makes the singular comment, found only in Mark, that Gehenna is "Where their worm does not die, and the fire is not quenched" (Mk. 9:48). The word worm signifies the process of unending corruption. Interpreters have at times understood "worm" as relating to the soul (the gnawings of conscience) and the fire which Jesus mentions in the context as referring to the body, but that is an overly precise distinction. Both metaphors come from the last verse of the great Book of Isaiah: "For their worm shall not die, their fire shall not be quenched, and they shall be an abhorrence to all flesh" (66:24). So terrible was this picture of judgment for the Jews, that when the passage was read in the synagogue the reader was obligated to repeat verse 23, which is a word of comfort, rather than close the lesson with this frightening word of judgment.

Hell is place of indescribable torment and distress. In the words of John R. W. Stott,

> Hell is a grim and dreadful reality. Let no man deceive you. Jesus spoke of it. He often called it "outer darkness," because it is infinite separation from God who is light. It is also called in the Bible "the second death" and the "lake of fire," terms which describe (no doubt symbolically) the forfeiture of eternal life and the ghastly

thirst of the souls which are involved in irrevocable banishment from God's presence.[19]

That this doctrine is unpalatable to many who bear the name of Christ can be seen from the attempts to water down the plain teachings of the Bible on this subject.

Wrong Views of Eternal Punishment
Annihilationism

Some Bible readers understand words such as death, destruction, perdition, and loss as meaning the cessation of existence. The biblical expression of fire, when used of hell, is interpreted by them to mean destruction once and for all.

Some Seventh-Day Adventists contend that God will ultimately blot out sin and sinners. Jehovah's Witnesses also deny the reality of hell, but hold that physical death means total destruction. The fire of Gehenna, they say, symbolizes annihilation. The founder of the Jehovah's Witnesses movement, Charles Russel, gave up church at the age of 17, primarily because of its teaching on hell. He taught that the wicked would be completely annihilated, for it was impossible, he thought, for a God of love to condemn people to eternal torment. But the impulse for this understanding of Scripture comes not from the Bible but from human speculation, and betrays a misunderstanding of biblical language. And even if it were granted that the ungodly are annihilated, that too would be a frightening prospect.

Universalism

The view that the punishment of the condemned is not eternal, but temporary and remedial, is as old as the third-century theologian Origen. It is known in theological jargon as the doctrine of *apokatastasis*, meaning the "restitution of all things" (an expression found in Acts 3:21). The teaching has several forms of expression. One is that death produces a change of character in the ungodly. Another is that suffering in hell leads people to turn from their sins. This form is more popular.

As in all heresy, Scripture is used to support this understanding of punishment. Acts 3:21 does indeed speak of the "restitution of all things." That cannot mean the salvation of all humanity, for two verses farther along (3:23) Peter warns that "every soul that does not listen to that prophet shall be destroyed from the people."

Universalists appeal also to Ephesians 1:10, where the gathering together of all things in heaven and earth in Christ is mentioned. While the verse does teach that in Christ all discordant elements of the universe are done away, it does not say that all will be saved eventually.

Another favorite is 1 Corinthians 15:22, "For as in Adam all die, so also in Christ shall all be made alive." The "all" in the second clause seems to refer to believers only, however, since in the context Paul is dealing with the resurrection of the saints. Should it be insisted that the "all" embraces all humanity, then nothing more is said than that they will all be raised, but not necessarily to eternal life, but rather as Jesus said, "to the resurrection of judgment" (Jn. 5:29).

Appeal is made also to God's desire that all people should be saved, as expressed in 1 Timothy 2:5 and 2 Peter 3:9. God's desire that everyone be saved does not mean, however, that all will be saved. That depends on each persons' response to Christ. Many passages in the New Testament speak of the universality of salvation, but they do not teach that all will be saved.

Besides using Scripture, restorationists employ arguments such as the following: 1. That eternal punishment contradicts the teaching of God's love. 2. That the grace of God knows no limits; it will continue to operate in the next world. 3. If souls were lost, God's triumph in Christ would not be complete. He would not be "everything to every one" (1 Cor. 15:28). 4. God is not only Judge, he is also Father, and no father could stand seeing one of his loved ones in agony forever. 5. That "eternal punishment" is remedial—a form of purgatory, as taught by the Roman Catholic Church.[20]

Appealing though such arguments may sound, they cannot be sustained by the teachings of the New Testament. Tasker warns that to thrust the severe passages to the side and "to concentrate solely upon passages of the gospel where the divine Fatherhood is proclaimed is to preach a debilitated Christianity, which does not and cannot do what Christ came into the world to do, viz. save men from the wrath to come."[21]

It should be pointed out that the adjective "eternal" (*aionios*), which some universalists understand as temporary, is applied not only to eternal death but also to eternal life (Mt. 25:46). If one eliminates eternal punishment then one must of necessity also eliminate eternal life. To be sure, the word "eternal" has a qualitative meaning, but the quantitative is thereby not denied. And that holds true also for the Greek idiom "for ever and ever" (*eis tous aionas ton aionon*). If the believers reign with Christ "for ever and ever" (Rev. 22:5), then we cannot take the word "age" (*aion*) and reconstruct it to mean a limited period when used of the punishment of the wicked.

God has done all he could for the salvation of humankind; he "gave his only Son, that whoever believes in him should not perish" (Jn. 3:16). There is deliverance from eternal doom, but we must meet God's condition: "Whoever believes in him." Today is the day of salvation. We do not know how long the patience of God will hold open the door of mercy to sinners. However, when the last day comes, the door will be shut. We dare not be kinder than God. "For his judgments are true and just" (Rev. 19:2).

In conclusion to this chapter on the fate of the ungodly, a few words should be said about the judgment of the righteous. While they have the assurance that they have not been appointed to wrath but to obtain salvation (1 Thess. 5:9), they too must appear "before the judgment seat of Christ, so that each one may receive good or evil, according to what he has done in the body" (2 Cor. 5:10).

Perhaps nowhere is the judgment of the saints described with such vivid metaphors as in 1 Corinthians 3:10-15. The service that one renders here in life is likened to a building which is built on the foundation Jesus Christ. While the quality of the foundation cannot be disputed, the materials we use in building on it may be either combustible (wood, hay, stubble) or durable (gold, silver, precious stones).

The day of judgment is likened to a fire which breaks out in a building. "The Day will disclose it, because it will be revealed with fire, and the fire will test what sort of work each one has done" (3:13). If the materials with which we build will stand God's test, we will receive reward. If, on the other hand, our work is burned up, we will suffer loss. Just what that means, Paul does not say. He makes it very plain, however, that the loss does not include the salvation of the believer. "He himself will be saved," like a man whose house burns to the ground and he escapes by the skin of his teeth. Salvation is by grace and not by works, but if we do not build properly we lose the reward of our labors.

It should not be overlooked that the fearful fate of the wicked is mentioned frequently in letters written to believers, and the import of that should not escape us. The Galatian believers are told that those who practice the works of the flesh "shall not inherit the kingdom" (Gal. 5:19, 20). The Corinthians are warned against unrighteousness in daily life for "the unrighteous will not inherit the kingdom of God" (1 Cor. 6:9). The Ephesian readers are warned against immorality, greed, and similar evils by a reminder that "it is because of these things that the wrath of God comes upon the sons of disobedience" (Eph. 5:6).

The author of the Epistle to the Hebrews warns his readers against apostasy, for it is, he says, "a fearful thing to fall into the hands of the living God" (Heb. 10:31). He exhorts them to "offer to God acceptable worship, with reverence and awe, for our God is a consuming fire" (12:28, 29).

Alan Richardson comments,

> By our acceptance of Christ in this day of opportunity we anticipate the verdict of the "last day" (Jn. 3:18; 12:48). We still must await

that verdict with fear and trembling (Rom. 2:6), not presuming upon the long-suffering goodness of God, putting our trust not in our own merits, but in Jesus who delivers us from the wrath to come (1 Thess. 1:10).[22]

Because of the love of God manifested in Jesus Christ we can have confidence on the day of judgment (1 Jn. 2:28; 4:17).

Discussion Questions

1. What is the origin of the Hebrew word *ge-hinnom* (Greek—*geena*)? Why did this infamous locality become a figure of speech to describe the place of eternal punishment?

2. There are numerous other figures in the New Testament to describe future damnation. What is the origin of Hades and Tartarus? How many different figures are used in 2 Peter 2:4-6? John uses three other figures in Revelation. Check them out in 11:7; 20:1; 19:20; 20:14; 20:10, and 21:8. Jesus, as reported by Matthew, uses still another image. Identify it by looking up Matthew 8:12.

3. What is the difference between the fire of judgment which the ungodly will be subjected to and the fire which Christians are subjected to in this life? Compare Matthew 18:9 and 1 Peter 1:7.

4. Why is wrath an essential characteristic of the personality of God? See Matthew 16:27 and Romans 1:18.

5. Can you identify two faulty views on eternal punishment? Some sincere Christians have espoused the view that ultimately all people will be saved. What arguments are used to support universal salvation? Do these Christians necessarily deny the reality of judgment and punishment? According to the author this interpretation of eternal punishment doesn't take into account all the teachings of the New Testament. Do you agree? Why?

6. Many writers and preachers have painted vivid pictures of hell for their audiences. In contrast, Helmut Thielicke, as quoted in this chapter, speaks about hell as separation from God, as being

"forced to see the glory of God and [yet] have no access to it."
What kind of language is appropriate for Christians who want to
impress upon the ungodly the judgment they'll face if they don't
repent and accept the gospel?

CHAPTER ELEVEN

"In My Father's House Are Many Mansions"

A question that naturally arises is, "Where on earth is heaven?"—as the title of a book puts it.[1] It should be said immediately that heaven cannot be located in the cosmic order as we know it, even though spatial categories such as "above" and "beneath" are used when speaking of the heavenly or demonic realm, respectively. Heaven is where God is. He was there long before he "created the heavens and the earth," and he will be there when this heaven and earth pass away.

When Christ appears at the end of this age, this present order shall disappear. "But the day of the Lord will come like a thief, and then the heavens will pass away with a loud noise, and the elements will be dissolved with fire, and the earth and the works that are upon it will be burned up" (2 Pet. 3:10). We look for new heavens and a new earth, says 2 Peter 3:13.

This sort of language already suggests that "heaven" has different meanings in the Bible. On the one hand, heaven together with earth is the Hebraic designation for this universe. Since the Hebrew word for heaven (*shamayim*) is always plural, it is often found as a plural in the Greek of the Septuagint and the New Testament. There was considerable speculation in Judaism on how many heavens there actually were. Some writers know of only one (Eth. Enoch, 4Esd., Syr. Bar.), others speak of three

(Test. Levi 2 f.), of five (Gr. Bar.), and still others of seven (Sl. Enoch, Test. Abr.). According to some, Paradise was located in the third heaven (S. Enoch 8:1-8; Ass. Ms. 37), others put it in the seventh. Paul, who reports an ecstatic vision in which he was caught up to the third heaven, identifies this heaven as Paradise (2 Cor. 12:2, 3).

This cosmic order, then, is comprised of "heaven and earth." But heaven sometimes means simply the sky. When Jesus exhorts us to look at "the birds of the heaven" (Mt. 6:26), means the "air," the "sky." However, when a few verses earlier he tells his hearers to "lay up for yourselves treasures in heaven" (Mt. 6:20), he obviously doesn't mean the sky. And when he reminds the triumphant seventy that they should rejoice rather that their names "are written in heaven" (Lk. 10:20) he has in mind a place that is "far beyond the starry sky."

Heaven is God's dwelling place. That is why he is called the "heavenly Father" (Mt. 6:14). So closely was heaven identified with God that "heaven" became a surrogate for God. This is reflected in the New Testament, for example, in the confession of the Prodigal, "Father, I have sinned against heaven [i.e. God] and before you" (Lk. 15:21).

Let us now turn to some of the images which the New Testament writers employ to describe heaven, God's dwelling place, the longed-for goal of the saints.

The Father's House

Our Lord comforted his disciples prior to his death with the words of assurance, "In my Father's house are many rooms" (Jn. 14:2). The Father's house is a reference to heaven, where God lives. What is meant by "rooms" *(monai)* is not so clear. The Vulgate has *mansiones*, from which the translators of the Authorized Version (1611) got the English "mansions." In Latin the word was used for temporary dwellings, leading some interpreters to suggest that the believers in the world to come would pass from one state to the next until the final goal—seeing God—was reached. Some expositors have understood the Greek word *mone* in a similar way; but by derivation (*meno*—to remain) the word means rather a permanent dwelling place. Today the English translation "mansions" conveys the notion of a stately home in heaven, but *mone* does not have that connotation however vast or glorious the heavenly "rooms" may be.

The sense of permanent residence is brought out clearly in verse 23—the only other occurrence of *mone* in the New Testament—where Jesus promises that God will make his permanent "abode" with those who love him. "Abode" is a bit archaic, as A. M. Hunter suggests,[2] and *The New English Bible* renders it as "dwelling-places," as in the hymn, "And in God's house for evermore, My dwelling place shall be." But the RSV's "rooms" is the briefest, and perhaps the best, translation.[3]

Compared with the transitory nature of this earthly life, these "rooms," which are fully equipped, are permanent dwellings. To go to the Father's house is to go "home" to be with the Lord. And whether we die before the coming of Christ (Phil. 1:23) or whether we participate in the Parousia (1 Thess. 4:17), in either case, we shall be with the Lord for ever. Hauck says, "The permanence, indestructibility and continuation of this union is expressed by *mone*."[4] Eviction from this home is impossible.[5] The fact that there are many "dwelling places" in the Father's house suggests that there is room enough for all who go there. Jesus added that he was going "to prepare a place" for us (14:2).

In 2 Corinthians 5:1 Paul compares this earthly tent in which we live at the present with the "building from God, a house not made with hands, eternal in the heavens." However, the context suggests that he has the heavenly "body" of the believer in mind, in contrast to his earthly body, and not the eternal dwelling place of the believers with God.

God's dwelling place in heaven is at times described in terms of a sanctuary. In Israel's sacred past God dwelt in a sanctuary in the midst of his people, and this earthly sanctuary was but a shadow of the heavenly (Ex. 25:8). Indeed the expression "my

Father's house" may be reminiscent of Israel's sanctuary. The writer to the Hebrews explains that Christ has entered into a sanctuary not made by hands, "but into heaven itself, now to appear in the presence of God on our behalf" (Heb. 9:24). This sanctuary in heaven is called the "true tent which is set up not by man but by the Lord" (Heb. 8:2).

In several visions of the other world which John, the Seer of Pamos, had, God's dwelling place in heaven is described also as a sanctuary (cf. Rev. 8:1-5; 11:19; 15:5). More often, however, John describes God as the one who is seated on his throne. Particularly significant is the throne-room vision recorded in chapters 4 and 5. The many-colored lights which flash from the throne, reflected in the "sea of glass," create an overwhelming sense of the transcendence and majesty of God and the glory of his dwelling place.

In chapter 7 John sees the saints, who come home to glory from great tribulation, stand before the throne of God and serve him in his temple (7:15). Here the heavenly sanctuary and the throne-room seem to have merged. Moreover, he goes on to say that the One "upon the throne will shelter them with his presence" (v. 15). The promise that God will tabernacle over his own in glory would evoke memories of God's tent in the wilderness. "For the tabernacle to be *over* his people is a way of saying that the immediate presence of God will shelter and protect them from all that would harm Is. 4:5, 6)."[6]

God's tent recalls the wilderness journey when Israel lived in tents. By contrast heaven is described as "eternal habitations" (Lk. 16:9). This is a word of Jesus following the exhortation to make friends with the mammon of unrighteousness "so that when it fails they may receive you into the eternal habitations." Michaelis points out that it makes no difference whether we understand this to be a reference to the failure of mammon, of death, or of the end of the world, the "eternal huts" of this saying are unquestionably to be understood eschatologically.[7] Whether the "they" (in "receive") refers to angels, or to friends we have made with our mammon, or whether the plural means "God" in keeping with the Jewish tendency to avoid the use of his name, the saints will be welcomed into the Father's house when the great Day comes.

Paradise

Paradise is a borrowed word of Persian origin and is used in Genesis 2:8 ff. (Septuagint) of primeval Eden. The word itself means a garden, an orchard or park, and came to be used of the place of bliss in the world to come.

In Judaism there was much speculation on what happened to the original paradise of Genesis 2 and 3. Because of Adam's sin it was now hidden. Some located it in the third heaven (Ap. Mos. 37:5; Sl. Enoch 8:1). One view was that it was the dwelling place of the righteous in the intermediate state. So paradise became another name for the abode of the blessed after death. In the renewed creation it was to emerge from concealment and become the dwelling-place of the righteous.

In the New Testament the word occurs only three times. In Luke 23:43 Jesus promises the penitent robber fellowship with him in paradise that very day. That seems to suggest that Jesus used the word for the intermediate state; however, it may well be a reference to the place of eternal bliss. According to the Testament of Levi (18:10), Messiah was expected to "open the gates of paradise."[8]

In 2 Corinthians 12:4 Paul speaks of being caught up into paradise where he heard words "which man may not utter." Paradise is used here as a parallel to "the third heaven" (v. 2). Evidently Paul, by an ecstatic experience, was given a glimpse into the heavenly world.

In Revelation 2:7 the Spirit promises the church of Ephesus: "To him who conquers I will grant to eat of the tree of life, which is in the paradise of God." Adam and Eve were barred from the tree of life when they sinned. The overcomer receives back what original man lost, but much more: this tree stands in the heavenly paradise. The paradise of God in Revelation symbolizes the eschatological state in which God and man are restored to that perfect fellowship which existed before the entrance of sin into the world.

In the last chapter of the Revelation John picks up the paradise motif and combines it with Ezekiel's vision of the healing waters flowing from the temple (Ezek. 47:12). Earlier, Ezekiel has prophesied; "This land that was desolate has become like the garden of Eden" (Ezek. 36:35). That promise is fulfilled in the end. The Seer has a vision of a river of water of life flowing from the throne of God. This river symbolizes the fullness of the life-powers which flow through paradise.

On either side of this crystal stream stood the tree of life bearing fruit continuously (Rev. 22:1, 2). Its rich fruit and its healing leaves indicate the complete absence of physical and spiritual want in the world to come. The tree of life was a regular feature in Jewish pictures of paradise (cf. 2 Esdr. 8:52; 2 Enoch 8: 3, 4). To eat of the tree of life means to live for ever without need or want.

On the whole the New Testament writers do not make much use of the term paradise. The reason may be that the emphasis in the New Testament lies not so much on the place of future bliss as on being with Christ for ever. Not the place but the Person makes paradise a true "garden of God."

Abraham's Bosom

In the parable of the rich man and Lazarus, Lazarus is carried by angels to Abraham's bosom (Lk. 16:22, 23). This is a well-known expression in Judaism used to describe the bliss of the righteous in the hereafter.[9] The word bosom *(kolpos)* actually refers to the fold of a loose garment rather than the breast and can stand for the person. It is a pictorial expression to indicate the loving relationship between people, derived from the love of a mother who holds her child in her lap (Luther used *"Schoss"*). The word is used to describe the intimate relation of the Son to his Father (Jn. 1:18). At the Last Supper John lay at Jesus' bosom (Jn. 13:23), indicating a tender relationship between the two. To be carried to Abraham's bosom, then, indicates the tender love awaiting the righteous after death.[10]

There is, however, another nuance to this metaphor. In the light of John 13:23, where John lies next to Jesus at the table, we should perhaps think of Lazarus sitting at table with Abraham. "In the first instance we are to think in terms of the feast of the blessed at which Lazarus takes the place of honour."[11] To sit at table with someone, in oriental practice, indicates friendship and closeness. Perhaps the table scene in heaven is deliberately contrasted with the table on earth where Lazarus got only the crumbs which came from the rich man's table. Now at Abraham's table he enjoys a rich banquet.

Jesus, complaining about the lack of response to his message in Israel, foresaw the day when many would come from east and west and sit at table with Abraham, Isaac, and Jacob in the kingdom of heaven while the sons of the kingdom would be cast into outer darkness (Mt. 8:11, 12). The many from east and west are the Gentile believers who will enjoy the messianic banquet.

The messianic banquet motif runs right through the New Testament. One reason Jesus refused to make bread out of stones was to reject current messianic notions. It was expected that when Messiah came men would hunger and thirst no more; Messiah would supply bread. This explains in part at least, why they wanted to make Jesus king after he had fed the multitude in the wilderness (Jn. 6:15). And when Jesus declared at the Last Supper that he would not drink again of this fruit of the vine until that day when he would drink it new with them in the Father's kingdom (Mt. 26:29), he pointed to the eschatological banquet which was to be celebrated in the world to come.

In Revelation 19 John describes the bliss of the redeemed in terms of a great wedding feast in which the Lamb and his bride celebrate their union. Whereas the marriage metaphor is more prominent here than the banquet motif, one cannot think of one without the other. There is no suggestion here that heaven will be an orgy of sensual delights—as some religious thinkers have described it. The bride is attired in fine linen, bright and pure. The wedding feast speaks of eternal joy and fullness in the presence of Christ.

The City of God

Perhaps there was no word that evoked so many sacred associations in the mind of a Jew as did Jerusalem. To begin with Jerusalem possessed no advantages. It was located in the Judean mountains and was not a trade route. Until the time of David Jerusalem was simply a Jebusite settlement which meant nothing to the faith of the Israelite tribes. But because of its neutral position and location, David made it the capital and so the promises of God to David and his house became linked to Jerusalem. The "holy city," the "mountain of Yahweh," became the bearer of all expectations for the future and was the sign of God's faithfulness to his chosen people.

When Jerusalem was destroyed by the Babylonians, the hope was expressed that a new Jerusalem would be established some day and its glory would outshine the former city (Is. 54:11-15; 65:17-25). In Judaism the hopes of an eschatological Jerusalem were quite diverse. Some thought of it as a heavenly city but felt this city could not come until the earthly Jerusalem was established. Others thought of it as coming down from heaven to earth. Still others saw it as a heavenly city only.

It need not surprise us, therefore, that Jerusalem becomes the city for which the saints on earth wait. Of Abraham, the prototype of the Christian pilgrim, it is said that he lived in tents, "For he looked forward to the city which has foundations, whose builder and maker is God" (Heb. 11:10). The author of Hebrews of course, has the heavenly Jerusalem in mind.[12]

Since all the great gifts of salvation are experienced proleptically here on earth, the same writer, in Hebrews 12:22-24, says of the believers that they "have come to Mount Zion and to the city of the living God, the heavenly Jerusalem, and to innumerable angels in festal gathering, and to the assembly of the first-born who are enrolled in heaven." The new Jerusalem has not yet come down to men, but by conversion to God, believers already have access to it. They have become citizens of this city with foundations for which Abraham looked. Here on earth they have no lasting city, but they "seek the city which is to come" (Heb. 13:14). However, by faith they are members of the heavenly city.

If the movable tabernacle in the wilderness was built according to the pattern of the heavenly, we can understand why in Judaism the city of Jerusalem and its temple were thought of as copies of the heavenly archetypes. Christians, however, viewed the earthly Jerusalem in a rather different light. Stephen, the first Christian martyr, following in Jesus' footsteps, saw Jerusalem and its temple, theologically at least, as *passé*.

Paul went so far as to identify the Jerusalem that he knew with Mount Sinai—the symbol of bondage to the law. In contrast to the "now" Jerusalem, he identifies the "above" Jerusalem as the city of the free and says, "She is our mother" (Gal. 4:25, 26). He doesn't speak of the "upper" Jerusalem as the one that is yet to come, since he wants to stress the present reality of the city of which all the saints are members. "Thus there is in the concept of the New Jerusalem, both with Paul and the author of Hebrews, a peculiar relationship of tension, in which the church must live."[13]

In Revelation 3:12 the overcomer is given the promise that God will write on him "the name of my God, and the name of the city of my God, the new Jerusalem which comes down from my God out of heaven." The meaning is that the faithful belong to God and hold citizenship in the new Jerusalem, God's dwelling place. This city is on the heavenly Mount Zion. John, in a vision, sees those who have God's name on them coming home to Mount Zion, where they join with the saints of all the ages in songs of triumph (Rev. 14).

Earthly Jerusalem with its temple lay in ruins when John wrote. Moreover, the resistance of Judaism to the Christian gospel, and the sufferings which believers had to endure at the hands of unbelieving Jews, led John to identify Jerusalem with Sodom and Egypt (Rev. 11:2, 8)—symbols of wickedness and enslavement. Because earthly Jerusalem had been so polluted, it was to bear the shameful designation of "the great city," which links it with Babylon, the city of harlots (11:8; 14:8; 16:19; 17:18). Nations shall trample on it throughout the end times (42 months). There is, of course, always hope for Israel, for even some from the "synagogue of Satan" will respond to the church's witness (Rev. 3:9).

Finally John sees "the holy city, new Jerusalem, coming down out of heaven from God, prepared as a bride adorned for her husband" (Rev. 21:2). Against the backdrop of the destruction of Babylon, the citadel of evil and oppression (Rev. 18), the new Jerusalem appears in all its splendor and glory. The new Jerusalem is the new world in concrete form.

There was a time when this biblical language was taken literally. This led to the drawing of pictures and maps of the new Jerusalem. But this "celestial geographizing," as it has been called, violates the use of symbolic language, which is designed to be evocative, as hymns and poems are. John nearly breaks the bonds of language to describe what he saw in the vision.

What gives this city its felicity is the fact that God dwells there with his people (21:3). Moreover, all the evils and sorrows that attend life here on earth will be absent there (21:4). Like the inner sanctuary of the temple (1 Kings 6:20) this city is shaped like a perfect cube. This signifies that the city is a holy place because God lives there, but also that it is the epitome of perfection. The city is said to be 12,000 stadia (1,500 miles/2,419 kilometers) in every direction, symbolizing its vastness (there will be room for all), its perfection, and its splendor.

The radiance of the city is likened to a glittering gem. There is complete security in this city—it has walls around it, guarded by angels (21:12, 13). The wall is jasper, the streets of the city are of pure gold, clear as glass. The foundations of the wall are adorned with every imaginable jewel. The wall defines the city's boundary; it indicates what's in and what's outside. These are of course metaphors taken from this earth to convey something of the incomprehensible glory of this heavenly city. "As the eternal dwelling place of God and his people, it is described in language which continually attempts to break free from its limitations in order to do justice to the reality it so imperfectly describes."[14]

John's real interest is not the glory of the holy city as such, but the fact that God's people dwell in this unspeakable splendor in the presence of God. This is underscored by the fact that the names of the 12 tribes are written on the gates and those of the 12 apostles on the foundations (21:12-14). In Israel there was always the hope that the lost tribes of the northern kingdom would be restored in the end times (4 Esd. 13:39 ff.; Apc. Bar. 78:1 ff.), but for John this nationalistic hope has retreated into the background. The twelve tribes and the twelve apostles represent the entire people of God—all of them saved by the blood of the Lamb.

Since the throne of God and the Lamb are found in this city (22:1-5), his saints shall reign for ever. That they reign with Christ for ever does not imply that there are people over whom they reign. It simply means that they participate in the triumph of the Lamb in God's eternal kingdom.

Paul, writing to Timothy, declares, "If we endure, we shall also reign with him" (2 Tim. 2:12). He is confident that God will rescue him from every evil and save him for his "heavenly kingdom" (4:18). To the overcomer Christ holds out the privilege of sitting with him on his throne, just as he has conquered and sat down with the Father on his throne (Rev. 3:21). That promise is fulfilled in the new city, where the saints rule with Christ forever.

The pictures of heaven in this chapter have their background either in the Old Testament or in Jewish apocalyptic. Under the inspiration of the Spirit the New Testament writers transmuted them and recast them. These heavenly pictures convey to the saints on earth something of that indescribable glory which "no eye has seen, nor ear heard, nor the heart of man conceived, what God has prepared for those who love him" (1 Cor. 2:9).

Discussion Questions

1. There are many biblical images for heaven. A number of them are listed below. Texts where they can be found are listed to the right, though they are scrambled. Look up each of the texts and match them with the pictures of heaven to the left.

Rooms	Mt. 26:29
House not made with hands	Lk. 16:9
Sanctuary	Lk. 23:43; Rev. 2:7
Tabernacle	Heb. 8:1, 2; Rev. 7:15
Throne of God	Heb. 9:24
Eternal tents or habitations	Heb. 11:10
Paradise	Rev. 3:12
Abraham's bosom	Rev. 7:15
Banquet or feast	Rev. 21:1, 2
City of God	Jn. 14:2
New Jerusalem	2: Cor. 5:1
Holy City	Lk. 16:22, 23

2. Many of these images had roots either in the Old Testament or Jewish apocalyptic writings. Using the author's explanations, what were the origins of these terms? How does each help to embellish the biblical concept of heaven? What is the central idea conveyed by each?

3. One of the insights of the writer to the Hebrews is that believers already have access to the city of God, even though they still live here on earth (Heb. 12:22-24; 13:14). What does it mean for the Christian to live in the world, yet have citizenship already in the kingdom to come? What kinds of tensions and conflicts does that create?

4. Note how many of these heavenly images are political terms. This would include throne of God, city of God, new Jerusalem, and holy city. Does this not imply that the Christian's allegiance to political realms in this world must always be subordinate to allegiance to God's kingdom?

CHAPTER TWELVE

"The Glory That Is to Be Revealed to Us"

It has been suggested that one reason the Bible has relatively little to say about heaven is that Christians do not want to be accused of preaching "pie in the sky." However, while the word "heaven" may not occur in any great abundance, references to the glory that is to be revealed to us in the age to come are found throughout the New Testament. The doctrine of heaven is woven through the fabric of Christianity. There is "pie in the sky"—an idiom which is completely foreign to the New Testament, of course—and we must not shy away from proclaiming this great truth. If proclaimed properly it becomes a good tonic for our souls.

If we daydream about heaven all the time to the point where we lose interest in the work of God's kingdom here on earth, then we are suffering from a kind of "homesickness" for heaven which is unhealthy. On the other hand, Paul exhorts us to set our minds "on things that are above" (Col. 3:2). In our secular society, the temptation to be earthly minded and to pursue worldly, temporal things is probably a greater temptation for us than to dwell too much on the heavenly world.

Since the time of our earthly sojourn is but a fleeting moment in comparison to the eternal state, we quite obviously want to be informed as best we can about the life in the world to come.

In our previous chapter we focused on the heavenly abode of the saints. The question that remains is whether something more can be said about that glory that shall be revealed to us when the new age dawns and the present order passes away. We want to be cautious, and not say more than the New Testament would allow us to say; on the other hand, we would certainly want to affirm everything that it teaches about the heavenly country for which we wait. For a biblical writer there was probably nothing that could surpass the wonder and the glory of seeing God—known in the language of theology as the *Visio Dei*.

The Visio Dei

It has been the hope of God's people throughout the ages that they might have the privilege of seeing God. "To see God" is a pictorial expression indicating the bliss of fellowship with God in his eternal kingdom.[1] In Judaism it was held that the vision of God was not possible in this life; it was reserved for the hour of death or for the age to come.[2] When Moses, the great lawgiver of the old dispensation, asked for the privilege of seeing God, he was told: "You cannot see my face; for man shall not see me and live" (Ex. 33:17-20). He was allowed to see only God's back (33:23). But even to get only a glimpse of God often proved to be a shattering experience for saints of both Old and New Testament (see, e.g., Isaiah 6:5 and 2 Corinthians 12:1-4), for God "dwells in unapproachable light, whom no man has ever seen or can see" (1 Tim. 6:16).

"No one has ever seen God," says John, but "the only Son, who is in the bosom of the Father, he has made him known" (Jn. 1:18). And when Philip later asked, "Lord, show us the Father, and we shall be satisfied," Jesus explains, "He who has seen me has seen the Father" (Jn. 14:9). In the Person of Jesus those who were witnesses of his incarnation could see what God was like. But it was God incarnate, God in the flesh. It was not yet the beatific vision for which God's people yearn.

There is a seeing of God that is possible to the eyes of faith during our earthly sojourn. Paul prays for his readers that the eyes of their hearts may be opened (Eph. 1:18). Nevertheless, as long as we are in this earthly body we "walk by faith, not by sight" (2 Cor. 5:7). Peter explains that even though we do not yet see him we can rejoice (1 Pet. 1:8). However, we see only by means of "a mirror dimly" (1 Cor. 13:12), not clearly, not yet face-to-face.

The promise of Jesus, that the pure in heart shall see God (Mt. 5:8), has not yet been completely fulfilled. It will be fulfilled only when the Lord comes. "We know that when he appears," says John, "we shall be like him, for we shall see him as he is" (1 Jn. 3:2). "To see the Lord," says Bruce, "is the highest and most glorious blessing that mortals can enjoy, but the beatific vision is reserved for those who are holy in heart and life."[3]

In the last chapter of the Bible the Seer of Patmos wraps up his great book of comfort with the assurance: "They shall see his face" (Rev. 22:4). All the bliss of eternity seems to be condensed in that phrase. What we see dimly in this life with the eyes of faith will be fully manifest when we see "face facing face" *(prosopon pros prosopon,* 1 Cor. 13:12).

A. M. Hunter observes:

> To behold the God before whom angels veil their faces, the God who created us and, in Christ, redeemed us, who so loved his lost and wandering children that he came right down among us to show us what he is like and then died on a Cross to save us from our sins and make us heirs of life eternal, and, beholding him, to behold all things in him and in the light of his redemption, this truly "were a well spent journey, Though seven deaths lay between."[4]

Glorification

To see God is to see his glory. The Hebrew word for glory *(kabod)* originally meant "weight," but it came to signify "worth," "wealth," "power," "dignity," "majesty" and "honor." As applied to God it signified his manifest brightness in power and holiness. " 'Glory' throughout the Old Testament often bears this theological meaning of God in his visible self-manifestation."[5]

This Hebrew understanding of glory was passed on to its Greek translation *doxa* (which to begin with meant "opinion"—as in orthodox—or "reputation").

To see the brilliant majesty of God in the midst of his people brings about their transformation. We have an illustration of this in the Exodus story. When Moses came down from the mountain on which God had spoken to him, his face shone so brightly that Israel could not look at him and he had to put a veil over his face when he spoke to the people (Ex. 34:29-35). Unfortunately, being a man of flesh and blood, this glory did not last; it faded.

The believer, says Paul, can look at Christ with unveiled face—the veil of unbelief having been removed—and by beholding him is transformed from one glory to another. This transformation is made possible by the Lord who is the Spirit (2 Cor. 3:18). "In sanctification, through the operation of the Holy Spirit who enables the believer constantly to behold the glory of the Lord, that image is increasingly imparted to the Christian."[6] Both the beholding (the verb *katoptrizo* can also mean "reflecting") and the being transformed are in the present tense, indicating a progressive transformation from glory to glory.

However, this is not yet the beatific vision, for we see Christ only "as in a mirror." We are still in the flesh and our vision is marred. And while the glory of Christ reflected in us, be it ever so dimly, is not fading, it is not yet that blaze of glory which Peter says "is to be revealed" when Christ returns (1 Pet. 5:1). That which made Isaiah the prophet cry out in despair when he saw the temple filled with the glory of God (Is. 6:1 ff.), will become for the saints the source of overwhelming joy. The holy city, as John saw it in a vision, is lit up with the glory of God (Rev. 21:11, 23).

"Sharing God's glory is one of the most frequently repeated idioms used to describe the final destiny of the redeemed."[7] Jesus prayed that the Father would grant his followers to see the glory which he had before the foundation of the world (Jn. 17:24). And Paul is certain that just as Christ was glorified after his passion, we shall be "glorified with him" (Rom. 8:17). The writer to the Hebrews explains that it was fitting that Christ should be made perfect through suffering, since he has become the pioneer of our salvation and now brings many sons to glory (Heb. 2:10). When he appears we "will appear with him in glory" (Col. 3:4). Indeed Christ is our only "hope of glory" (Col. 1:27). "Participation in *doxa*," says Kittel, "whether here in hope or one day in consummation is participation in Christ."[8]

At the present the Christian life is characterized by suffering. But as Paul explains, "the sufferings of this present time are not worth comparing with the glory that is to be revealed to us" (Rom. 8:18). Or, to put it somewhat differently, the present affliction, which is momentary, "is preparing for us an eternal weight of glory [it should be remembered that the Hebrew word "glory" to begin with meant 'weight'] beyond all comparison" (2 Cor. 4:17). "Christian suffering . . . when compared with the everlasting ages of the glory to which it is leading is but a passing moment; affliction for Jesus' sake, however, crushing as it may seem, is in fact light, a weightless trifle, when weighed against the mass of that glory which is the inheritance of all who through grace have been made one with the Son of God."[9]

Through sin man has come "short of the glory of God" (Rom. 3:23), but God in his mercy has called us through the gospel to "obtain the glory of our Lord Jesus Christ" (2 Thess. 2:14). Not only initially did we hear the call of the gospel, which is a call to eternal glory, but God keeps on calling us to "his own kingdom and glory" (1 Thess. 2:12). The believer, therefore, can rejoice in his "hope of sharing the glory of God" (Rom. 5:2; 1 Pet. 4:13). Ladd says that " 'glory' comes to be the sum and substance of eschatological expectations."[10]

The glory that shall be ours at Christ's coming is an "eternal glory" (1 Pet. 5:10; 2 Tim. 2:10). That makes the sufferings of this life appear but a little while. "When the chief Shepherd is manifested," says Peter, "you will obtain the unfading crown of glory" (1 Pet. 5:4). Glory will be the reward for faithfulness to Jesus. And that leads us to say something about rewards.

Rich Rewards

The promise of rewards is not an insignificant aspect of
teaching. When we say that one of our loved ones has gone
or her reward, we are in good biblical tradition. Jesus pr
those who gave alms and who prayed in sincerity a rev
heaven (Mt. 6:3, 4). He assured those who sacrificed hou
lands, kith and kin, for the cause of Christ, that they would
without wages (Mt. 19:29). Paul explains that each man's
will be according to his labor (1 Cor. 3:8). In fact every good
that we do will be rewarded (Eph. 6:8), for God is not unju
he should overlook our work and our love for others (Heb. 6:10).

This strand of teaching has not always been appreciated, for
it seems to suggest that we can earn merits with God—a notion
only too common in Judaism. However, Jesus in one of his parables makes it plain that we have no right to claim rewards from
God. In the parable of the laborers in the vineyard (Mt. 20:1-16)
each man, those who came early as well as those who came late,
received a *denarius*. This did not appear just and fair to those who
worked all day. And that is the point of the parable. The rewards
of the kingdom are to be measured by God's grace.[11]

In the parable of the last judgment (Mt. 25:31-46) those who
are given entrance into the eternal kingdom turn out to be such
who have helped and served the needy with no thought of
recompense. Paul speaks "the reward . . . of grace" (Rom. 4:4), in
contrast to the reward of works, and that probably captures the
heart of this truth. All rewards spring from God's generous love
and are given by grace.

Another way of speaking of rewards in the age to come is in
terms of "treasure in heaven." Treasures on earth usually
consisted of costly clothing in oriental practice. Unlike earthly
treasures, which are consumed by moths, and which thieves can
steal, treasures in heaven are exempt from corrosion and decay
and beyond the reach of thieves. The concept "treasures in
heaven" is thoroughly Jewish (Test. of Levi 13:5; Ps. Sol. 9:9).[12]
The rich young man is told to sell all and he will have treasure in

heaven (Mk. 10:21). The rich fool laid up treasures on earth only, but in the end lost everything. "So is he who lays up treasure for himself, and is not rich toward God" (Lk. 12:21).

Related to the concept of treasure in heaven is that of "inheritance." Paul says that the Holy Spirit is God's down payment, as it were, of that inheritance which we shall possess some day (Eph. 1:14). Indeed he prays that the eyes of the saints be opened so that they might get a glimpse of "the riches of his glorious inheritance in the saints" (Eph. 1:18). In contrast to the inheritance of the land in the old covenant—an inheritance which Israel lost when enemies came into the land—the mediator of the new covenant has assured us of an "eternal inheritance" (Heb. 9:15). This inheritance is in heaven and so it is "imperishable, undefiled, and unfading" (1 Pet. 1:4). It is kept securely for us, as we are carefully guarded through faith for the salvation that is to be revealed in the last day.

Among the rewards which Jesus promises his followers in the age to come is "eternal life" (Mt. 19:29).

Eternal Life

This term occurs some 17 times in John's Gospel. It is relatively rare in the Synoptics or, for that matter, in other New Testament writers. In many cases, however, the simple word "life" has the same meaning as "eternal life." The concept of eternal life is foreign to the Old Testament, where little is known about the life in the world to come (Daniel 12:2 is the only exception).

In intertestamental Judaism, "eternal life" (or simply "life") comes to be used for the life of the resurrection (Ps. Sol. 3:16; 1 Enoch 37:4; 40:9; Test. Asher 5:2). When the dualism of "this age" and the "age to come" merged, the rabbis frequently spoke of the "life of the age to come."[13] This is also one of its primary meanings in the New Testament.

The rich young ruler asked Jesus: "Good Teacher, what must I do to inherit eternal life?" (Mk. 10:17; Mt. 19:16; Lk. 18:18). "To inherit" is used here in the sense of future possession. The questioner, while confused on how to obtain eternal life, clearly thinks of life in the age to come. This becomes even more obvious in Jesus' comments on the difficulty which the wealthy have in entering the kingdom of God (Mk. 10:23), and the promise of eternal life "in the age to come" (v. 30) to those who forsake everything for Jesus' sake.

This futuristic meaning of eternal life is found also in the Fourth Gospel, although John has a tendency to stress the present aspect of eternal life. He who sees the ripe harvest "gathers fruit for eternal life" (4:36). Life in this world stands in contrast to eternal life, that is the life in the age to come (Jn. 12:25). And in the familiar Gospel text, John 3:16, eternal life stands in opposition to eternal ruin.

As with other gifts of salvation, there is both an "already" and a "not yet" about eternal life. Jesus foresaw the hour when the dead would hear the voice of God's Son and some would come forth unto eternal life (Jn. 5:28, 29). That is clearly futuristic. On the other hand, he says, that "he who believes in the Son has eternal life" (Jn. 3:36). That's a present possession. In his first epistle John stresses that it is possible for the believer to know here and now that he has eternal life (1 Jn. 5:13, 20). But eternal life is experienced in the present only as a foretaste, it is properly a blessing for the age to come. In that respect it is like the kingdom of God which Jesus brought and which is present today, but which is yet to come.

One fundamental aspect of the meaning of eternal life is that it is endless. There is, however, another dimension to this concept. Eternal life is qualitatively different from the present, physical life. The life of man outside of Christ is fleshly *(kata sarka)*, the life in Christ is spiritual *(kata pneuma)*. The former leads to death (Rom. 5:14; 6:21; 7:5), the latter is a priceless good, not only because it is everlasting (Rom. 5:10, 21; 1 Cor. 15:19; Col. 3:4),[14] but also because it is "real life" (1 Tim. 6:19).

Whereas we have a foretaste of this life in the present, eternal life lies beyond the final judgment of humankind, and stands in stark contrast to eternal death. To live in the future age is not simply to carry on from this present age, but to pass successfully the great day of judgment, receiving the gift of eternal life.

There are hardly any definitions or descriptions of eternal life in the New Testament; the emphasis lies rather on the conditions for obtaining it. Eternal life cannot be earned; it must be received as a gift (Rom. 6:23). On the other hand, it must be laid hold of (1 Tim. 6:12).

There is nothing humanity desires more than life. However, endless life here on earth in a body that is beset with weaknesses in an evil age that is full of trials and temptation is not a very glorious prospect. But to live eternally with God in the age to come, where all the trammels of earthly existence are done away with, is a kind of shorthand for all that we could ever wish or think.

Rest from Labors

The rest (*anapausis*—refreshment) which Jesus promised those who take up his yoke of discipleship (Mt. 11:28-30) is but a foretaste of the rest that awaits God's children in the next world.

No New Testament writer has developed this theme as extensively as the writer to the Hebrews (3:18—4:11). After reviewing the history of Israel's rebellion following the Exodus, he explains that God swore that those who were unbelieving should not enter his rest. But the entry into the land of Canaan did not exhaust the promise of rest. "For if Joshua had given them rest, God would not speak later of another day" (4:8). There is then a rest still awaiting the new people of God, which they must press on to enter.

This rest is called "God's rest" not only in the sense that he promises it, but also in the sense that he enjoys rest and offers to share it with his people. This rest can be experienced proleptically by all those who hear the gospel while the day of salvation lasts.

Also, in the age to come there will be rest from all tribulation which the believer has to suffer in this age. Paul writes to the Thessalonians that when Christ returns he will "repay with affliction those who afflict you," and "grant rest with us to you who are afflicted" (2 Thess. 1:6, 7).

The word for rest which Paul uses here is *anesis*, meaning relief and relaxation, freedom from restraint and tension (as the slackening of a taut bowstring). To all those who suffer for the cause of Christ the promise of rest is not a selfish hope. Paul himself has this hope, indeed the phrase "with us" suggests that he is speaking out of his own difficult situation. In one sense God recompenses his children who are asked to suffer for his name by giving them the peace that comes from the assurance of his presence in the darkness of this age. But in a fuller sense rest is available to the saints in the age to come.

In the Apocalypse John hears "a voice from heaven saying, 'Write this: Blessed are the dead who die in the Lord henceforth.' 'Blessed indeed' says the Spirit, 'that they may rest from their labors, for their deeds follow them.' " (Rev. 14:13). Faithfulness to Christ often calls for martyrdom, but the dead in Christ are blessed, for they enter into eternal rest. This second of seven Beatitudes in the Revelation stands in sharp contrast to the judgment which apostates are to suffer.

For some modern readers this prospect of rest has less meaning than for some of our ancestors whose life was much more filled with heavy work, sickness, and sorrow. Not rest but meaningful activity is what we desire. To that it may be said that we should not think of rest in heaven as condemnation to eternal inactivity. However, little is said about work in heaven since work as man knows it here in life stands under the sign of the curse (Gen. 3:17 ff.). For the readers of the Revelation the promise of the rest was extremely meaningful.[15]

However, the prospect of rest should be balanced by the other biblical models of waking up to a new day (1 Cor. 15:51, 52; 1 Thess. 4:14). "The parousia will not close the era of divine creativity, for God is the living God, and where there is life there is happening. God will yet work fresh wonders beyond our present imaginings."[16]

That "heaven is not a place of indolent leisure, but a place where service is done"[17] must also be emphasized. When John says that in the paradise of God "his servants shall worship him" (Rev. 22:3), he assures us of meaningful existence. Our experiences with worship on earth leave much to be desired, and therefore the thought of worshiping God, or serving God, throughout eternity may not hold any great attraction for us. But it should be remembered that man was created to serve and to worship God. Through the fall this goal was thwarted, but in the eternal kingdom, the deepest desires and longings of the human heart will be fulfilled in the service of God.

Unspeakable Joy

The note of joy is struck everywhere in the New Testament from the outbursts of song at the birth of Jesus to the hallelujah choruses of the Apocalypse. "Joy is experienced through the salvation achieved by Jesus Christ in the past, personally experienced in the present, and confidently expected in the future."[18] Even in the present those who suffer for Jesus' sake can rejoice because their reward is great in heaven (Mt. 5:12; 1 Pet. 1:8).

In the parable of the talents the good and faithful servants "enter into the joy" of their Lord (Mt. 25:21, 23)—a kind of alternative to eternal life or heavenly kingdom. Jude praises him "who is able to keep you from falling and to present you without blemish before the presence of his glory with rejoicing" (v. 24). *Agalliasis*, "exceeding joy," "is essentially a word that belongs to heaven."[19]

Peter calls upon the church to look away from its sufferings, which he says are insignificant compared with rejoicing which will break forth at the end of time (1 Pet. 1:8; 4:13).

In John's vision of the saints coming home to Mount Zion, after suffering great tribulation, he sees God ready to welcome them, and like a mother with handkerchief in hand, he wipes every tear from their eyes (7:17; cf. 21:4). And when the marriage supper of the Lamb is announced John hears the voice of vast multitudes saying, "Let us rejoice and exult and give him the glory, for the marriage of the Lamb has come" (19:7).

What makes the joy of heaven so indescribably wonderful is the fact that all those things which cause us grief in this life will not be found there. Some of the most moving pictures of heaven are drawn in negatives rather than in positives. There will be no more hunger or thirst (Rev. 7:16)—imagery slightly more striking for Near Eastern man in the first century than for affluent Americans in the twentieth. What is more: "Death shall be no more, neither shall there be mourning nor crying nor pain" (Rev. 21:4). Weeping may last for the night, but joy comes in the morning!

Discussion Questions

1. The author makes a distinction between the vision of God believers have in this life and the beatific vision they will experience in the life to come. What is the difference? What kind of vision of God is being spoken of in the following texts? 1 Timothy 6:16; Ephesians 1:18; 1 Corinthians 13:12; Matthew 5:8; 1 John 3:2; Revelation 22:4. What does it mean to behold the glory of God? See 2 Corinthians 3:18; 1 Peter 5:1; Revelation 21:11, 23; Romans 18:17, 18; Colossians 3:4. Can you identify with Paul's assertion that the sufferings of this life are greatly overshadowed by the glory which we will experience in the life to come?

2. Heavenly rewards have been downplayed by some Christians, says the author. Why? Nonetheless, rewards are a part of the biblical testimony as evidenced by these texts: Matthew 6:1, 2; 1 Corinthians 3:8; Ephesians 6:8; Romans 4:4. On what basis will these rewards be given?

3. Another aspect of the heavenly vision is that believers will experience "release from labors." What kind of labor is intended by this phrase? See especially Hebrews 3:18—4:11. What experiences in life have you had which made you long for this release from labors?

4. The concept "eternal life" is almost completely unique to which Gospel writer? Does eternal life refer only to future, unending life? Or does it also carry the idea of a special quality of life here on earth? See John 3:16, 36; 4:36; 5:28, 29; 1 John 5:13, 20. What does it mean that followers of Christ can already experience a foretaste of this eternal life here and now? In what ways does this eternal life set Christians apart from unbelievers?

5. If Christians have the hope of unspeakable joy in the future, should that not lend a touch of joy to the life of Christians in the world? Why are some Christians unjoyful? Someone has said, "Joy is an infallible sign of the presence of God." Do you agree?

CHAPTER THIRTEEN

"Waiting for That Blessed Hope"

For the Greek in Paul's day hope was "a phantom figure, delusive and dangerous, making sport of human life, and recklessly leading men on by glimpses of the unattainable."[1] The world outside of Christ is described by Paul as "having no hope" (Eph. 2:12), particularly in the face of death (1 Thess. 4:13). That is not to say that unbelievers do not have aspirations, dreams, and desires which they hope to see fulfilled in their lives. The old Latin adage, *Dum spiro, spero* ("while I breathe, I hope") is just as true of them as it is of Christ's followers.

Indeed, occasionally the word "hope" is used by the biblical writers in that natural, human sense. When Paul says that "the plowman should plow in hope and the thresher thresh in hope" (1 Cor. 9:10), he uses the word without any peculiarly Christian sense. But if there is no hope beyond death, then we must use the word "hope" with reservation, knowing full well that it is not really hope. Therefore, we must distinguish clearly between earthly hopes, desires, or wishes and what Paul calls "the blessed hope."

The Christian hope is not to be confused with blithe optimism. It carries a more profound cargo. Interestingly the word *elpis* ("hope") is never used in the plural in the New Testament—not "hopes" but "hope" characterizes the life of the believer. The blessed hope is wide enough to embrace all the hopes of the believer in his daily life; indeed, it undergirds them. Christian hope does not have its roots in the changing circumstance of life in which hopes and dreams are often shattered and buried. Rather, it springs, first of all, from the deep conviction that God is the Lord of history. In spite of the vicissitudes of history and the enigmas and disappointments of life, he is leading his people to a glorious goal. This is what gave Israel such an indomitable hope. Even when circumstances were utterly bleak, there was always the conviction that God would break in at any time and usher in his reign.

For the Christian believer, however, there is another solid foundation for hope—that in Christ God has in fact intervened and brought in his kingdom. We don't see everything subject to him as yet, but it's only a matter of time when the kingdom will be revealed in all its splendor. This makes the Book of Revelation such an optimistic book, in spite of the fact that it opens up to us the depths of the demonic. Christ has conquered at the cross and through this bleeding Lamb the victory over all the Babylons of this world is finally established.

So central is hope in the theology of the New Testament that, together with faith and love, this trilogy is a kind of explication of the very essence of the Christian life (cf. Rom. 5:1-5; 1 Cor. 13; Eph. 4:1-6; 1 Thess. 1:3; 5:8).

It is fitting that we should conclude our study of the doctrine of future things by inquiring about the nature and the substance of the blessed hope and what it means to live by it. In the first part of the chapter we will restrict ourselves to the biblical texts which contain the word "hope" (*elpis, elpizo*), which restricts our study almost entirely to Paul, Peter, and the writer to the Hebrews. The concept of hope is obviously much larger and so in the second part of our study we shall draw upon other passages. Obviously we must be selective, for the blessed hope is woven into the warp and woof of the New Testament message as a whole. Wherever one opens its pages, the blessed hope is never far from the surface.

The Nature of the Blessed Hope

Descriptive Adjectives

A *Living Hope*. Peter blesses God who by his great mercy has born us "anew to a living hope through the resurrection of Jesus Christ from the dead" (1 Pet. 1:3). This living hope stands in contrast to earthly hopes, many of which go to the dust and die. G. F. Watts pictures Hope, his allegorical lady, as perched blindfolded on the rolling world, bowing over her broken lute to extract a melody from one remaining string. How typical of earthly hopes! So many hopes which we had as children have turned out to be pipe dreams. Many of the cherished hopes which we carried into life have been left unfulfilled. But the Christian hope is a "living" hope.

It is a living hope in that it does not fade away like earthly hopes. In ordinary life hope often proves vain and elusive, but "in the new life hope is 'living,' i.e., it is vigorous and cannot fail."[2] Or, to use Bo Reicke's words, "By 'living hope' is meant a hope by which one can live. It sustains the soul after the new birth with the nourishment needed for a higher life."[3]

The reason this hope is "living" is that it is bound to the risen Christ, who rose from the grave, having slain the enemy, Death, who grinds man's earthly hopes into the ground. Through the new birth we have been joined to Christ who "brought life and immortality to light," and so our hope remains alive; indeed, it enlivens us.

A *Good Hope*. In one of his prayers for the Thessalonians Paul writes: "Now may our Lord Jesus Christ himself, and God our Father, who loved us and gave us eternal comfort and good hope through grace, comfort your hearts and establish them in every good work and word" (2 Thess. 2:16, 17). The believer's hope is a good hope both in contrast with the empty hopes of those who are not believers, and also because it will endure till it is realized at the coming of Christ.[4] The lot of the early Christians was outwardly "of all men most miserable." But they had a good hope, and this sure confidence that their Lord would return to establish his reign and bring to an end all evil powers, completely transformed their lives. "Good hope" stands as a parallel to "eternal comfort," which points to the age to come when God will wipe away all tears. Because we have a good hope, this eternal comfort can be enjoyed in a small measure at least already here on earth. Both hope and comfort, says Paul, are given to us by the grace of God.

A Blessed Hope. "Awaiting our blessed hope, the appearing of the glory of our great God and Savior Jesus Christ" (Tit. 2:13). There is no question in this text what it is that the believer waits for. It is the appearing of Jesus Christ in glory. And the hope of his return is a "blessed" hope. The word "blessed" (*makarios*) means happy, felicitous, joyous. It is such a joyous hope that even in the midst of tribulation we can "rejoice in our hope of sharing the glory of God" (Rom. 5:2).

Striking Metaphors

Hope as an Anchor. So closely is the hope of the believer tied to the risen and exalted Christ that the writer to the Hebrews calls hope "a sure and steadfast anchor of the soul, a hope that enters into the inner shrine behind the curtain, where Jesus has gone" (Heb. 6:19 f.). That the writer should compare the Christian hope to an anchor, living as he did in the Mediterranean world where travel by sea was common, need not surprise us. Only twice does the word anchor occur in the New Testament: once in the sailor's chapter (Acts 28), where Luke recounts Paul's voyage to Rome, and in Hebrews 6:19. The word anchor (*agkura*—"hook") was well-known in the Greek world both in the literal sense and as a metaphor for that which is foundational in a person's life. And that is how the writer to the Hebrews uses it.

Eugene Nida describes the difficulty of translating Hebrews 6:19 into the language of desert dwellers in French West Africa who have never seen an ocean or sailed in a boat. To them, the word "anchor" has no meaning at all. They chose the term "picketting-peg"—used by the Mossi people to tie their horses to.

Hence the Mossi people read in their New Testament, "A strong and steadfast picketting-peg for the soul."[5]

The sacrificial work of Christ, completed when he ascended to heaven, is the anchor of our hope. "Christ's sacrifice, then, is an anchor which not only holds us in the storms of this world but ties and tethers us to the unseen one. We stand . . . between two worlds—the present one and the world to come. But the anchor of Christian hope, founded on Christ's sacrifice, penetrates the veil which separates the unseen world from our eyes and is fastened on the farther side."[6] Some day we will go to where Christ has gone, if we hold fast to that hope which is firmly anchored in the heavenly world.

Hope as a Helmet. Paul exhorts the Thessalonians to put on the breastplate of faith and love, and then—to round out the familiar triad—he adds: "And for a helmet the hope of salvation" (1 Thess. 5:8). Of all the pieces of armor worn by a Roman soldier, the helmet was of extreme significance, for it protected his head. The hope of salvation protects the believer from the deadly strokes of the enemy. It should be observed that salvation—deliverance—is both a present possession and a future hope. Here the future deliverance, which will take place when Christ returns, is in focus. The blessed hope serves the believer as a helmet to shield him from the attacks of the evil one to which the church is exposed throughout these "last days."

The Substance of the Blessed Hope

As we examine the texts which deal with hope, we notice that hope is thought of as a concrete heavenly reality. Hope does not describe our longings, but is a "hope laid up . . . in heaven" (Col. 1:5; cf. 1 Pet. 3:15). Christian hope is not grounded in something as fluctuating and uncertain as material circumstances; still less in moods, which change; but it is a heavenly treasure which nothing on earth can destroy.

Because hope has such an objective character, Paul can speak of "awaiting our blessed hope" (Tit. 2:13). In everyday life we may "wait" and we may "hope," but we do not speak of waiting for some hope. The Christian hope, however, has substance. Newbigin writes: "Christian hope is an utterly unshakable assurance of that which shall be, because God has promised it, which is sure even though our desire for it should faint and grow weary."[7]

Whereas the hope of the believer is, on the one hand, laid up in heaven, the writer of the epistle to the Hebrews (known for his many warnings) reminds his readers that this hope has to be seized; it must be laid hold of, and held firm. "We are his house if we hold fast [*katecho*—to hold down, or hold firm] our confidence and pride in our hope" (Heb. 3:6). The evidence that we are members of God's household is seen in our laying hold of our hope (cf. Heb. 6:11, 18; 10:23). Like all great gifts of redemption, there is a divine givenness which calls for our response.

That the blessed hope is not simply an undefined yearning can be seen by the elements which make up the substance of the blessed hope. We hope for the glory of God (Rom. 5:2; Col. 1:27); for adoption as sons (Rom. 8:23), for the redemption of our bodies (Rom. 8:23); for righteousness (Gal. 5:5); for salvation (1 Thess. 5:8); for eternal life (Tit. 1:2; 3:7); for the appearing of the Savior (Tit. 2:13; 1 Cor. 1:7; Heb. 9:28; 1 Thess. 1:10; Phil. 3:20); for a new heaven and a new earth (2 Pet. 3:13). This list can be extended. We give these examples only to show that there is nothing nebulous or amorphous about what the believer hopes for.

The blessed hope of the believer is intensely personal. The consummation of God's redemptive plan is to be understood in terms of personal reunion and loving fellowship with the Christ whom we have come to know through the gospel. "This means that when the Christian contemplates the future, he must not think primarily in terms of events and their relationships, or of provisions and their enjoyment, but his attention is to be fixed on Christ, and his joy is to be found in union with him."[8]

A question that naturally arises is whether this blessed hope has a firm foundation.

The Source and Foundation of the Blessed Hope

Writing to the Colossians Paul exhorts his readers to continue in the faith, "stable and steadfast, not shifting from the hope of the gospel which you heard" (Col. 1:23). Here the source of the believer's hope is said to be the *gospel,* which was received when it was heard. It is in the gospel that we are assured of God's love, manifested in the sacrifice of his Son, Jesus Christ. Christian hope must never be separated from that one great historical event which lies in the past, when God in Christ reconciled the world to himself. It is in the gospel that God extends his invitation to men and women to become members of his family, and so one might also say that God's *call* is the source of our hope.

In what appears to be an early Christian creed Paul lists "one hope" as an essential article in a seven-member confession. After "one hope" the apostle explains that it is "one hope that belongs to your call" (Eph. 4:4). God's call stresses God's initiative in our salvation. God called us by the gospel to become members of his kingdom, and the hope we now have springs from this gracious call of God. Earlier in the same epistle Paul prayed that God would open the eyes of the readers so that they might know what is the hope of their calling (Eph. 1:18). All of us need to discover the deeper meanings and implications of the Christian hope which we have.

Since Christ's death and resurrection is the very heart of the gospel, our hope can be said to have its source and ground in Christ's *saving work.* Our hope of salvation rests on the ground that Christ died for us; as a result we have the assurance that whether we live or die we shall live with him forever (1 Thess. 5:8-10). We recall that Peter in his first epistle attributes the living hope of the Christian believer to the resurrection of Jesus Christ (1 Pet. 1:3).

Since God by his grace has given us a good hope (2 Thess. 2:16), it could be said, also, that our hope rests entirely on *God* (1 Pet. 1:21; 1 Tim. 4:10). And the Holy Spirit in our lives assures us that this hope will not make us ashamed (Rom. 5:5). "The presence of the Holy Spirit is the link between the mighty work of God in the past, in which our hope finds its anchorage, and the future realization of it; it is the present guarantee of a great destiny yet to be entered into."[9]

Hope also comes from the *Scriptures*, since they witness to the saving acts of God in history. No doubt Paul had the Old Testament in mind when he reminded his Roman readers that they could have hope "by the encouragement of the scriptures" (15:4), but Christians in his day were already making Israel's sacred history their own. How often when hope burned dimly in a believer's heart, it was fanned into flame by a promise from the Word of God.

Looking at hope from a slightly different perspective, the writer to the Hebrews makes the Christian *faith* the foundation of the believer's hope. That seems rather precarious if faith is understood as something we do, but that evidently is not how the writer of Hebrews understood it. "Faith is the assurance of things hoped for, the conviction of things not seen" (Heb. 11:1). The Greek noun for "assurance" is *hupostasis,* meaning literally "that which stands beneath" and so comes to mean "foundation" or "support." In legal and commercial usage it carries the "real estate" meaning of property.[10]

Did the author of Hebrews mean that *faith* gave substance to our hope? Did he mean that faith makes us confident of what we hope for? A. M. Hunter suggests we take the legal meaning for "assurance," for in the papyri the word is used for legal documents bearing on the ownership of a piece of property—"title-deeds" we might say.[11]

Faith, then, may be thought of as the "title-deeds" of things hoped for. We have not yet seen our future inheritance, that "better country" (Heb. 11:16). But we have God's promise that one day we shall inherit our heavenly possessions (Eph. 1:14).

The practical question now is: How shall we live here on earth while we wait for the blessed hope, the appearing of our Lord and Savior Jesus Christ?

The Blessed Hope and Our Daily Life

Waiting and Working

When the blessed hope is understood correctly, it never leads to escapism or fatalism. Indeed, quite the opposite is the case. The deep assurance that God will lead history to a glorious consummation makes our work in this world meaningful and worthwhile. To "wait" for Christ's return means to "work." To expect a friend for dinner does not have to do so much with a mental state as doing the appropriate things in preparation for his coming. If we expect something unusually good to happen, we may not have an image of its occurrence lying in our mind; but we may be found humming a tune even though we are not thinking of the event itself.[12] So it is with the hope of Christ's return.

Jesus in his Olivet Discourse speaks of the servant whom his master sets over his household to give them food at the proper time. If, in the master's absence the servant faithfully performs his duties, he will be honored upon the return of the master. If, on the other hand, he thinks the master will be absent a long time and eats and drinks with the drunken and beats his subordinates, the master of that servant will come at an hour when he does not expect him and will punish him (Mt. 24:45-51; cf. Lk. 19:41-48). Whatever else this parable may teach, it certainly stresses the need for faithfulness in the work to which God has called us.

In the parable of the talents (Mt. 25:14-30) the master entrusted his property to his servants and then went away. "After a long time" the master returned to reward those servants who had been faithful stewards of their master's property and to punish the one who had done nothing with it. Again the need for faithful labor during our Lord's absence is stressed.

Paul concludes his long chapter on the hope of the resurrection at the coming of the Lord with the exhortation to the Corinthians: "Therefore, my beloved brethren, be steadfast, immovable, always abounding in the work of the Lord, knowing that in the Lord your labor is not in vain" (1 Cor. 15:58).

Where the blessed hope burns bright there will be a greater

urgency about evangelism and the many other kinds of work in God's kingdom. Only after the Great Commission has been completed will Christ return (Mt. 28:19, 20). The end will not come, Jesus explained in his Olivet Discourse, until the gospel has been preached to all nations (Mt. 24:14).

Ready and Watching

In speaking about his Parousia Jesus said it would be like in the days of Noah: they ate, drank, married and gave in marriage, until the day Noah entered the ark and they were swept away by the flood. Two men will be in the field; one will be taken, another left. Two women will be grinding at the mill, one is taken and one is left (Mt. 24:36-41). Since we do not know the hour of his coming, we must be ready when Christ calls. But what does that mean?

One of the words for Christian watchfulness is "wait." There are several Greek words translated in English by "wait." Jesus said his followers were to have their loins girt and their lamps burning and "be like men who are *waiting [prosdechomai*—to expect, to wait] for their master to come home" (Lk. 12:35, 36). Paul uses the same word in his letter to Titus: "Awaiting our blessed hope, the appearing of the glory of our great God and Savior Jesus Christ" (2:13). The Corinthians, the apostle said, were *waiting [apekdechomai*—await eagerly] "for the revelation of our Lord Jesus Christ" (1 Cor. 1:7). And to the Romans he confesses that "we ourselves, who have the first fruits of the Spirit, groan inwardly as we *wait* for adoption as sons, the redemption of our bodies" (8:23).

James compares the believer who anticipates Christ's return to the farmer who waits patiently [*ekdechomai*—to look forward, to expect] for the early and late rains to fall so that he might have a harvest (Jas. 5:7). Paul uses one other word for waiting found only in 1 Thessalonians 1:10, namely *anameno*, to anticipate, to wait for. All these verbs mean essentially the same thing, but the variety of verbs suggests the importance of the concept of "waiting" for Christ's return.

We should be very careful not to understand this waiting to mean idleness. Nor does it mean that we nervously read the world's time clock to see whether we can discover how close we are to the end. It means much rather to be spiritually alert, doing the Master's business.

This is underscored by the use of the words for "watchfulness." There are five Greek words in the New Testament translated by our English "watch." Two of these can be dismissed immediately *(tereo* and *paratereo)* since they are never used with reference to the Lord's return. One word that is used with reference to the Parousia *(nepho)* means literally to be sober, and not drunk. Metaphorically it signifies moral and spiritual alertness. Spiritual sobriety is a sign that we belong to the day (1 Thess. 5:6) and therefore will not be caught by surprise when the Lord comes as a thief in the night (1 Thess. 5:4). Several times Peter exhorts his readers to be "sober" in the light of Christ's appearing (1 Pet. 1:13; 4:7).

A fourth word *(agrupneo)*, means literally to keep oneself awake, and figuratively, to be on the alert. It is used several times in the Olivet Discourse (Mt. 13:13; Lk. 21:36) with reference to Christ's coming. The fifth and the most common of the five words translated as "watch" is *gregoreo*, which has essentially the same meaning as the previous word, and is found repeatedly in the mouth of Jesus (Mt. 24:42, 43; Mk. 13:34, 35, 37). "Let us keep awake *[gregoreo]* and be sober" (1 Thess. 5:6). One example comes from the last book of the Bible: "Lo, I am coming like a thief! Blessed is he who is awake, keeping his garments that he may not go naked and be seen exposed!" (16:15).

Twice Paul links with the word "hope" a rare Greek word *(apokaradokia):* "eager expectation" (Phil. 1:20; Rom. 8:19). It stresses the intensity of the forward look which is characteristic of the Christian. There are two ideas in the Greek word: first, awaiting with outstretched head; second, turning away from other objects—concentrated attention. It is the expectancy of the head outstretched, eagerly straining forward.[13]

To watch for the coming of the Lord, then, does not mean to get all excited, as did the Thessalonians, so that they began to neglect even their daily duties (1 Thess. 4:11, 12); it means to live soberly and to go about our tasks quietly. Nor does it mean that we live in constant fear that we might be caught unawares. It does not even mean that we constantly think or talk about the return of Christ (although the subject will never be far in the background); but it means that we live holy lives, for John says, "And everyone who thus hopes in him purifies himself as he is pure" (1 Jn. 3:3). Gundry points out quite correctly that "the purifying influence of the second coming does not lie in the fear of 'getting caught' at the unexpected moment of the Parousia, but in the fact that our whole life will pass in review before the Lord."[14]

The Bride who is prepared for the marriage supper of the Lamb is described as clothed in fine linen, bright and pure—this fine linen, the author explains, is the righteous deeds of the saints (Rev. 19:8). To be ready and watching means to be in right relationship with God and man; it means purity of life, faithful service; it means loyalty to Jesus in the trials of the last days; it means to live the pilgrim life.

Sojourners and Strangers

Israel had a long sojourner's tradition. When Abraham came into the promised land he was a stranger, a sojourner in the land of promise, as in a foreign land, living in tents (Heb. 11:9). Of his descendants the writer to the Hebrews says that they died without seeing the promise fulfilled and "having acknowledged that they were strangers and exiles on the earth" (11:13).

This "pilgrim" tradition of the Old Testament people of God becomes a prototype in the New Testament of the Christian sojourner. The word pilgrim reminds us too much of the many who make journeys to sacred shrines. Pilgrimages to the Holy Land in our day are often a sign of our material affluence, for we can always return to our comfortable homes. Paul Minear (in a class lecture) suggested that a modern equivalent for the New Testament

concept of the "pilgrim" is the word "refugee" who has no homeland. Where believers are conscious of living in the last hour they
confess with the writer of the Epistle of Diognetus (second
century) that "every foreign land is our homeland and every
homeland is our foreign land" (5:5).

New Testament believers are described as "temporary
residents" (*parepidemoi*) and "resident aliens" (*paroikoi*). Both
words have the preposition *para* in them, indicating that they are
"para-citizens" in this world. They live in the world, but are not of
it. For that reason Peter exhorts his readers as "aliens and exiles to
abstain from the passions of the flesh that wage war against your
soul" (1 Pet. 2:11). Their life must reflect their true homeland; it
must set them off from those who are simply "earthdwellers."

The German scholar, K. L. Schmidt, who wrote an outstand-
ing article on "sojourner" for the *Theological Dictionary of the
New Testament,* incurred the wrath of the Nazis in the thirties.
He was deposed from his professorial chair in Vonn, stripped of
his citizenship, and expelled from his fatherland, so that when he
had finished his article on the Christian 'pilgrim' he had become
one himself.[15]

Twice in the New Testament believers are addressed as
people who live in the "dispersion" (*diaspora*) (1 Pet. 1:1; Jas.
1:1). The word was used for Jews who lived outside Palestine, the
homeland of Israel. So the church is scattered all over the world,
but its true fatherland is in heaven (Phil. 3:1, 9); not earthly
Jerusalem, but "the Jerusalem above is free, and she is our
mother" (Gal. 4:26).

"Christian faith must not be presumptuous. It should not
embrace the mood of one who has already arrived at his final
destination. It should be marked by the mood of pilgrimage,
travel, exodus, openness, expectation, change, readiness, even
unrest."[16] It is because we have no abiding city here on earth,
since we seek the one which is to come, that the writer to the Hebrews calls us to go forth outside the camp to bear abuse for
Christ's sake (Heb. 13:13, 14).

The call to Christians to be sojourners is not popular today. Should any church leader address a pastoral letter to a congregation as Peter did with the words: "To the exiles of the Dispersion" (1 Pet. 1:1), he would, to say the least, sound anachronistic. " 'Otherworldliness' has gone out of fashion, 'this worldliness' and 'with-itness' are everything."[17]

Since the form of this world is passing away, all of life's relationships must be tempered by this awareness (1 Cor. 7:29-31). Those who buy are to be as if they did not possess; those who use the world (as we all do) should not use it to the hilt. In patriarchal language we are called to a "tent-life" (Heb. 11:9). How else can we witness as they did "that they were strangers and exiles on the earth" (Heb. 11:13).

> Belief in the imminence of the parousia is not primarily a conscious mental state which has to be sustained with effort. It is a practical attitude. ... It is waiting on God and living life in a way which acknowledges his sovereignty as Lord over time, and which trusts him as the faithful One who will perform his promises. Such an attitude is neither peculiar to the first century nor obsolete now.[18]

Discussion Questions

1. Name some of the adjectives used to describe hope in the Bible. For help, look up 1 Peter 1:3; 2 Thessalonians 2:16, 17; Titus 2:13. What are some of the biblical metaphors for the Christian hope? See Hebrews 6:19 ff. and 1 Thessalonians 5:8.

2. What are some of the elements of the Christian hope? Consult Romans 5:2; 8:23; Galations 5:5; 1 Thessalonians 5:8; Titus 1:2; 2:13; 2 Peter 3:13.

3. What is the source and basis for the Christian hope? Some relevant texts are Colossians 1:23; Ephesians 4:4; 1 Peter 1:3, 21; Romans 5:5; 15:4.

4. What are we Christians to do in anticipation of Christ's coming and the hope that we have for the future? The author says that we are to *wait* and to *work*, and that these two concepts are

synonymous with each other. What does he mean by that? Look up these clues as to how the Christian should live in anticipation of God's future consummation: 1 Corinthians 15:58; Matthew 28:19, 20; Luke 12:35, 36; 1 Peter 1:13; 1 Thessalonians 4:11, 12; 1 John 3:3.

5. One New Testament scholar has said that the biblical image of the sojourner carries with it the idea of one who travels lightly; like a hiker, he can put all his earthly possessions into a backpack. Is the biblical injunction to be as sojourners and strangers in this world a judgment on the wealth of Christians in the United States and Canada?

6. What is the greater danger for the Christians you know: That they will become so heaven-oriented that they lose sight of God's purpose for them in this world? Or that they will become so secular that they lose sight of God's ultimate purpose which will be manifest in the age to come? What is the biblical antidote for an unhealthy otherworldliness? For an unhealthy this-worldliness?

End Notes

Preface

1. W. Dyrness, "The Age of Aquarius," in *Dreams, Visions and Oracles*, eds. Armerding and Gasque (Baker, 1977), p. 23.

Chapter One

1. F. F. Bruce, *Commentary on the Book of Acts, New International Commentary on the New Testament*, hereafter NICNT (Eerdmans, 1954), p. 68.
2. I. H. Marshall, *The Epistles of John, NICNT* (Eerdmans, 1968), p. 148.
3. *Ibid*, p. 148.
4. J. R. W. Stott, *The Epistles of John, Tyndale New Testament Commentary*, hereafter *Tyndale*. (Eerdmans, 1964), p. 148.
5. D. Hill, *The Gospel of Matthew, New Century Bible*, hereafter NCB (The Attic Press, 1964), p. 93.
6. F. F. Bruce, *The Epistle to the Hebrews, NICNT* (Eerdmans, 1964), p. 256.
7. Hanns Lilje, *The Last Book of the Bible* (Muhlenberg Press, 1957), p. 43.
8. R. Mounce, *The Book of Revelation, NICNT* (Eerdmans, 1977), p. 392.
9. H. Conzelmann, *The Theology of St. Luke* (Faber, 1960). "The main motif in the recasting to which Luke subjects his source proves to be the delay of the Parousia," (p. 131).
10. Clement's First Letter in *Early Christian Fathers*, ed. C. C. Richardson (The Macmillan Co., 1970), xxiii.
11. M. Green, *The Second Epistle of Peter and the General Epistle of Jude, Tyndale* (Eerdmans, 1968), p. 134.
12. I. H. Marshall, *Pocket Guide to Christian Beliefs* (IVP, 1978), p. 130.
13. A. C. Thisleton, "The Parousia in Modern Theology," in *Tyndale Bulletin* (21/1976), p. 51.

Chapter Two

1. W. Dyrness, in *Christianity Today* (Sept. 24, 1976), p. 19.
2. T. F. Glasson, *His Appearing and His Kingdom* (The Epworth Press, 1953), p. 44.
3. *Ibid.,* p. 45.
4. *Ibid.,* p. 45.
5. *Ibid.,* p. 48.
6. *Ibid.,* p. 59.
7. Alexander Reese, *The Approaching Advent of Christ* (Kregel, 1975), p. 241.
8. C. R. Taylor, *Jesus Is Coming Soon!* (Today in Bible Prophecy, 1975), p. 89.
9. D. Guthrie, *The Pastoral Epistles, Tyndale* (Eerdmans, 1957), p. 91 f.
10. M. Green, *Second Peter,* p. 93.
11. Justin, *Dialogue,* li.
12. I. H. Marshall, *Pocket Guide to Christian Beliefs,* p. 129.
13. O. Cullmann, *The Early Church* (SCM Press, 1956), p. 157.
14. G. E. Ladd, *The Last Things* (Eerdmans, 1978), p. 28.
15. C. S. Lewis, quoted in *Dreams, Visions and Oracles,* eds. Armerding and Gasque, p. 37.

Chapter Three

1. H. Thielicke, *Between Heaven and Earth* (Harper and Row,1965),pp.185ff.
2. J. R. W. Stott, *Christian Counter-Culture* (InterVarsity Press, 1978), p. 53.
3. F. F. Bruce, *Paul: Apostle of the Heart Set Free* (Eerdmans, 1977), p. 139.
4. F. Hauck, *"hypomone,"* in *Theological Dictionary of the New Testament* hereafter *TDNT* (Eerdmans, 1964-74), eds. G. Kittel and G. Friedrich VIII, 585.
5. P. Beyerhaus, "Interpreting the Signs of the Times," *Christianity Today* (April 13, 1973), p. 56.
6. See also Ted Rendall, "Preparing Today for Persecution Tomorrow," *Prairie Overcomer* (August 1978), pp. 432-33.
7. *Ibid.,* p. 432 f.
8. R. Gundry, *The Church and the Tribulation* (Zondervan, 1973).
9. G. E. Ladd, *The Last Things,* p. 64.

Chapter Four

1. G. Carey, *I Believe in Man* (Eerdmans, 1977), p. 161.
2. O. Cullmann, "Death," *Interpreter's Dictionary of the Bible* hereafter *IDB* (Abingdon, 1962), ed. G. Buttrick, I, 807.
3. Carey, *op. cit.,* p. 163.
4. R. V. G. Tasker, *The Second Epistle of Paul to the Corinthians, Tyndale* (Eerdmans, 1958), p. 78.
5. G. E. Ladd, *The Last Things,* p. 30.
6. Emil Brunner, *Eternal Hope* (The Westminster Press, 1954), p. 108.
7. E. E. Ellis, "2 Corinthians 5:1-10 in Pauline Eschatology," *New Testament Studies,* VI (1959-60), 211-224.

8. N. E. Dahl, *The Resurrection of the Body* (SCM Press, 1962), p. 78.

9. G. E. Ladd, *The Last Things*, p. 37.

10. F. F. Bruce, "The Idea of Immortality in Paul," in *A Companion to Paul* (Alba House, 1975), ed. M. J. Taylor, p. 131.

11. G. E. Ladd, *A Theology of the New Testament* (Eerdmans, 1974), p. 553.

12. O. Cullmann, *The Early Church* (SCM Press, 1956), p. 148 f.

13. H. Ridderbos, *Paul: An Outline of His Theology* (Eerdmans, 1975), p. 507.

14. A. M. Hunter, *Gleanings from the New Testament* (The Westminster Press, 1975), p. 131.

Chapter Five

1. T. F. Glasson, *The Second Advent* (The Epworth Press, 1963), p. 188.

2. I. H. Marshall, *The Epistles of John*, p. 71.

3. L. Morris, *The Epistles of Paul to the Thessalonians*, NICNT (Eerdmans, 1960), p. 221.

4. A. L. Moore, *The Parousia in the New Testament* (E. J. Brill, 1966), p. 113 f.

5. G. E. Ladd, *The Blessed Hope* (Eerdmans, 1956), p. 95.

6. T. F. Glasson, *His Appearing and His Kingdom* (The Epworth Press, 1953), p. 36.

7. *Ibid.*, p. 59.

8. R. L. Cox, "Will the Real Antichrist Please Stand Up!" *Eternity* (May 1974), pp. 15 ff.

9. P. Althaus, *Die Letzten Dinge* (C. Bertelsmann, 1949), p. 286.

10. Emil Brunner, *Eternal Hope*, p. 80.

Chapter Six

1. A. Oepke, "parousia," *TDNT*, IV, 859-60.

2. W. F. Arndt, and F. Wilbur Gingrich, *A Greek-English Lexicon* (Chicago University Press, 1957), s.v.

3. A. Reese, *The Approaching Advent of Christ* (Marshall, Morgan & Scott, n.d.), p. 19.

4. G. E. Ladd, *The Last Things*, p. 56.

5. W. Lane, *The Gospel According to Mark*, NICNT (Eerdmans, 1975), p. 476.

6. E. Peterson, "apantesis," *TDNT*, I, 380-381.

7. M. Rissi, *The Future of the World* (Alec R. Allenson, 1966), p. 18.

8. R. Mounce, *The Revelation*, p. 349.

9. R. Longenecker, "The Return of Christ," in *Dreams, Visions and Oracles*, p. 149.

Chapter Seven

1. G. E. Ladd, *The Last Things*, p. 81.

2. F. F. Bruce, *Paul: Apostle of the Heart Set Free*, p. 303.

3. *Ibid.*, p. 76.

4. G. E. Ladd, *The Last Things*, p. 74.

5. Karl Heim, *The Church of Christ and the Problems of the Day* (Scribner's, 1935), p. 157.

6. F. F. Bruce, *Paul: Apostle of the Heart Set Free*, p. 305.
7. *Ibid.*, p. 301.
8. A. M. Hunter, *Gleanings from the New Testament*, p. 159.
9. N. E. Dahl, *The Resurrection of the Body*, p. 94.
10. *Ibid.*, p. 15.
11. F. W. Dillistone, *C. H. Dodd* (Eerdmans, 1977), p. 237.

Chapter Eight

1. J. R. W. Stott, quoted in *Mennonite Brethren Herald* (Aug. 20, 1976), p. 17.
2. E. Lohse, *"chilios," in TDNT*, IX, 466-471.
3. M. Rissi, *The Future of the World*, p. 34.
4. T. F. Glasson, *His Appearing and His Kingdom*, p. 38.
5. M. Rissi, *op. cit.*, p. 36.
6. R. G. Clouse, *The Meaning of the Millennium* (InterVarsity, 1977), p. 11.
7. T. F. Glasson, *op. cit.*, p. 129.
8. Justin, *Dialogue with Trypho*, p. 80.
9. For a recent statement of the various millennial views see M. J. Erickson, *Contemporary Options in Eschatology* (Baker, 1977).
10. F. F. Bruce, *Answers to Questions* (Zondervan, 1973), p. 228.
11. G. E. Ladd, in *The Meaning of the Millennium*, ed. by R. G. Clouse, p. 39.

Chapter Nine

1. H. Buis, *The Doctrine of Eternal Punishment* (Presbyterian and Reformed, 1957), p. 27.
2. E. Hennecke-W. Schneemelcher, *The New Testament Apocrypha* (Westminster Press, 1965), "Apocalypse of Peter," II, 672 ff., "Apocalypse of Paul," II, 755 ff.
3. A. Richardson, *An Introduction to the Theology of the New Testament* (Harper and Row, 1954), p. 75.
4. R. V. G. Tasker, *The Biblical Doctrine of the Wrath of God* (Tyndale, 1951), p. 37.
5. For more details see C. H. H. Scobie, *John the Baptist* (Fortress Press, 1964).
6. Richardson, *op. cit.*, p. 77.
7. J. W. Wenham, *The Goodness of God* (InterVarsity, 1974), p. 41.
8. H. L. Strack and P. Billerbeck, *Kommentar zum Neu Testament aus Talmud und Midrasch* (Beck, 1922-61), II, 465.
9. F. F. Bruce, *1 and 2 Corinthians*, NCB (The Attic Press, 1971), p. 206.
10. C. Pinnock, "Why Is Jesus the Only Way?" *Eternity* (12/1976), p. 13.
11. I. H. Marshall, *Pocket Guide to Christian Beliefs*, p. 136 f.
12. M. Green, *The Second Epistle of Peter and the General Epistle of Jude*, p. 119.

Chapter Ten

1. A. Monod, quoted in R. Pache, *The Future Life* (Moody Press, 1962), p. 295.
2. J. R. W. Stott, *Chritian Mission* (InterVarsity, 1975), p. 113.

3. J. Jeremias, *"geenna," TDNT*, I, 657 f.

4. G. R. Beasley-Murray, *The Book of Revelation*, *NCB* (The Attic Press, 1974), p. 304.

5. D. Hill, *The Gospel of Matthew*, p. 159.

6. H. Conzelmann, *"skotos,"* in *TDNT*. VII. 423 f.

7. H. T. Bryson, *Yes, Virginia There Is a Hell* (Broadman Press, 1975), p. 14.

8. H. S. Hahn and C. Brown, in *Dictionary of New Testament Theology*, I, 112.

9. G. Staehlin, *"Orge,"* in *TDNT*, V, 422.

10. L. Morris, *The Apostolic Preaching of the Cross* (Eerdmans, 1955), p. 162.

11. F. Filson, *St. Paul's Conception of Recompense* (J. C. Hinrichsche, 1931), p. 40, n. 2.

12. G. E. Ladd, *The Last Things*, p. 89.

13. F. Filson, *op. cit.*, p. 48.

14. H. Theilicke, *The Waiting Father* (Harper and Brothers, 1959), p. 48.

15. R. Mounce, *Revelation*, p. 94.

16. A. Opeke, *"apollumi," TDNT*, I, 396.

17. H. C. Hahn, in *Dictionary of New Testament Theology*, I, 466.

18. K. H. Rengstorf, *"brogmus," TDNT*, I, 642.

19. J. R. W. Stott, *Basic Christianity* (Eerdmans, 1971), 2nd. ed., p. 74.

20. See W. Barclay, *A Spiritual Autobiography* (Eerdmans, 1975), where he sets forth his reasons for holding to universalism.

21. Tasker, *Wrath of God*, p. 36.

22. A. Richardson, *Theology of New Testament*, p. 78.

Chapter Eleven

1. A. E. Travis, *Where on Earth Is Heaven?* (Broadman Press, 1974).

2. A. M. Hunter, *Probing the New Testament* (John Knox Press, 1972), p. 64.

3. *Ibid.*, p. 64.

4. F. Hauck, *"meno,"* in *TDNT*, IV, 580.

5. Tasker, *The Gospel According to St. John* (Eerdmans, 1961), p. 171.

6. R. Mounce, *Revelation*, p. 175.

7. W. Michaelis, *"skene,"* in *TDNT*, VII, 378.

8. H. Bietenhard and C. Brown, in *Dictionary of New Testament Theology*, II, 762.

9. R. Meyer, *"kolpos,"* in *TDNT*, III, 825.

10. J. Motyer, in *Dictionary of New Testament Theology*, I, 240.

11. R. Meyer, *op. cit.*, p. 825.

12. F. F. Bruce, *The Epistle to the Hebrews*, p. 298.

13. M. Rissi, *The Future of the World*, p. 40.

14. R. Mounce, *op. cit.*, p. 383.

Chapter Twelve

1. D. Hill, *The Gospel of Matthew*, p. 113.

2. Strack-Billerbeck, *op. cit.* I, 207 ff.

3. F. F. Bruce, *The Epistle to the Hebrews*, p. 365.

4. A. M. Hunter, *Probing the New Testament,* p. 157.
5. G. E. Ladd, *I Believe in the Resurrection* (Eerdmans, 1975), p. 119.
6. P. E. Hughes, *Paul's Second Epistle to the Corinthians, NICNT* (Eerdmans, 1962), p. 120.
7. G. E. Ladd, *op. cit.,* p. 118.
8. G. Kittel, *"doxa," in TDNT,* II, 250.
9. Hughes, *op. cit.,* p. 157.
10. G. E. Ladd, *op. cit.,* p. 119.
11. A. M. Hunter, *op. cit.,* p. 46.
12. D. Hill, *op. cit.,* p. 142.
13. G. E. Ladd, *Theology of the New Testament,* p. 255.
14. O. Piper, "Life," in *IDB,* III, 129.
15. W. Strawson, *Jesus and the Future Life* (Westminster Press, 1949), p. 185.
16. U. Simon, *Heaven in the Christian Tradition* (Harper and Brothers, 1958), p. 233.
17. A. C. Thistleton, "The Parousia in Modern Theology," *Tyndale Bulletin* (26/1976), p. 29.
18. E. Beyreuther, in *Dictionary of New Testament Theology,* II, 354.
19. M. Green, *Second Peter and Jude,* p. 121.

Chapter Thirteen

1. R. N. Flew, *Jesus and His Way* (The Epworth Press, 1963), p. 97.
2. E. Best, *1 Peter, NCB,* (The Attic Press, 1971), p. 76.
3. Bo Reicke, *The Epistles of James, Peter, and Jude, Anchor Bible* (Doubleday, 1964), p. 79.
4. L. Morris, *Thessalonians, NICNT,* p. 242.
5. E. A. Nida, *God's Word in Man's Language* (Harper and Brothers, 1952), p. 46.
6. Hunter, *Probing* p. 132.
7. L. Newbigin, in *Missions Under the Cross* (Edinburgh House Press, 1953), ed. N. Goodall, p. 108.
8. R. N. Longenecker, "The Return of Christ," in *Dreams, Visions and Oracles,* p. 146.
9. C. F. D. Moule, *The Meaning of Hope* (Fortress Press, 1953), p. 36.
10. A. M. Hunter, *op. cit.,* p. 133.
11. *Ibid.,* p. 134.
12. A. C. Thistleton, "The Parousia in Modern Theology," p. 53.
13. Flew, *op. cit.,* p. 101.
14. R. Gundry, *The Church and the Tribulation,* p. 40.
15. A. M. Hunter, *op. cit.,* p. 138.
16. A. C. Thistleton, *op. cit.,* p. 47.
17. A. M. Hunter, *op. cit.,* p. 138.
18. A. C. Thistleton, *op. cit.,* p. 53.

Index of Scriptures

David Ewert was born in Russia five years after the Communist Revolution. His family moved to Western Canada in the late 1920s, eventually settling on a farm. There David received his elementary education and began Bible studies in a local Mennonite Bible institute.

Ewert is professor of New Testament at Mennonite Brethren Biblical Seminary, Fresno, California. He teaches Greek language and exegesis as well as New Testament theology. For nineteen years he taught at Mennonite Brethren Bible College, Winnipeg, Manitoba, and for three years at Eastern Mennonite Seminary, Harrisonburg, Virginia. He also served as visiting professor at Union Biblical Seminary, Yeotmal, India; Regent College, Vancouver, British Columbia; and Associated Mennonite Biblical Seminaries, Elkhart, Indiana.

Because of his German-speaking ability, Ewert has been on preaching missions to congregations in Germany, Austria, and Switzerland, and has taught courses for ministers' retreats at Bienenberg, Switzerland. He has also served among German-speaking congregations in Brazil and Paraguay.

Ewert earned degrees at the University of British Columbia (BA), Central Baptist Seminary (BD), Wheaton College (MA), Luther Seminary (MTh), and McGill University (PhD). His books, published in English and German, include *How Our Bible Came to Us* (1976) and *Die Wunderwege Gottes mit der Gemeinde Jesu Christi* (1979). He has written numerous articles for Mennonite publications.

David Ewert is married to Lena Hamm, who was also born to German-speaking immigrant parents. They have five grown children, four daughters and one son. The Ewerts are members of the Butler Mennonite Brethren Church, Fresno, California.